Bolivia

Bolivia

BY BYRON AUGUSTIN

Enchantment of the World
Second Series

Children's Press®

A Division of Scholastic Inc.

NEW YORK TORONTO LONDON AUCKLAND SYDNEY
MEXICO CITY NEW DELHI HONG KONG
DANBURY, CONNECTICUT

Frontispiece: Rich vegetation of the Yungas region

Consultant: Louis R. Sadler, Ph.D., is a Latin American historian and heads the Department of History at New Mexico State University

Please note: All statistics are as up-to-date as possible at the time of publication.

Visit Children's Press on the Internet: http://publishing.grolier.com

Book Production by Herman Adler Design

Library of Congress Cataloging-in-Publication Data

Augustin, Byron
   Bolivia / by Byron Augustin.
      p. cm. — (Enchantment of the world. Second series)
   Includes bibliographical references and index.
   Summary: Describes the geography, history, plants and animals,
economy, language, religions, culture, and people of Bolivia.
   ISBN 0-516-21050-5
   1. Bolivia—Juvenile literature [1. Bolivia.] I. Title.
II. Series.
F3308.5.A94 2001
984—dc21
                                                           00-038316

   2 3 4 5 6 7 8 9 10 R 10 09 08 07 06 05 04 03 02 01

Acknowledgments

I would like to acknowledge my wife, Rebecca, who supported this project with patience and understanding and who also edited the text. I am indebted to Mauricio and Lorena, who traveled with me throughout Bolivia for two weeks. They served as wonderful travel companions, provided many insights into the culture and history of their country, and secured critical literature and data from the Bolivian government. I also appreciate the efforts of my editor, Halley Gatenby, who defines the word *professional*. This book is for the Torrez family, Noel Kempff, and the people of Bolivia.

Contents

Cover photo:
A mestizo woman
of La Paz

Deep valleys of the Yungas

An Indian woman and her alpaca

Jewel of the Andes

8

Bolivia is South America's best-kept secret, partly because the country is "landlocked." Bolivia has no direct access to the sea. Also, its rugged mountain terrain and thick tropical rain forests have made transportation difficult and contributed to Bolivia's isolation. However, international air travel is now helping to open the country to the rest of the world. Visitors are now discovering what Bolivians have always known—Bolivia is the "Jewel of the Andes." It is a country of diverse natural and cultural treasures.

Opposite: **The vast Altiplano lies between ranges of the Andes Mountains.**

Thin Air

In many respects, Bolivia is two countries. The western third of the nation is located at an average elevation above 12,000 feet (3,658 meters). It consists of the rugged ranges of the Andes Mountains and one of the world's great plateaus—the Altiplano. The air is thin, with reduced oxygen, which makes breathing difficult for first-time visitors. Tourists can visit the world's highest ski resort at 18,438 feet (5,620 m). Or, they can play golf on the world's highest golf course near La Paz. At this high altitude, golfers regularly hit drives of more than 300 yards (274 m).

Driving a ball on the world's highest golf course

The city of La Paz and
Mount Illimani

Most of Bolivia's people live in the highlands, with the highest density around the La Paz–Lake Titicaca region. Older colonial cities such as Potosí, Sucre, and Oruro are also located in the highlands. This region was once the source of rich mineral deposits, which were plundered by the Spanish conquistadores. The mines of Potosí were said to have produced enough silver to build a bridge from South America to Spain. Today, many of those mines are exhausted. High unemployment in the highlands is forcing many families to move to the lowlands.

Exotic Lowlands

The eastern two-thirds of Bolivia presents a totally different environment. Flat to gently rolling, Bolivians call it the Oriente. Here, the land is closer to sea level with elevations of 500 to 1,000 feet (152 to 305 m). The climate is tropical and semitropical. Rain is more abundant, temperatures are warmer, and the landscape is a lively green. Thousands of plant and animal species provide an exciting change from the bleak, gray Altiplano.

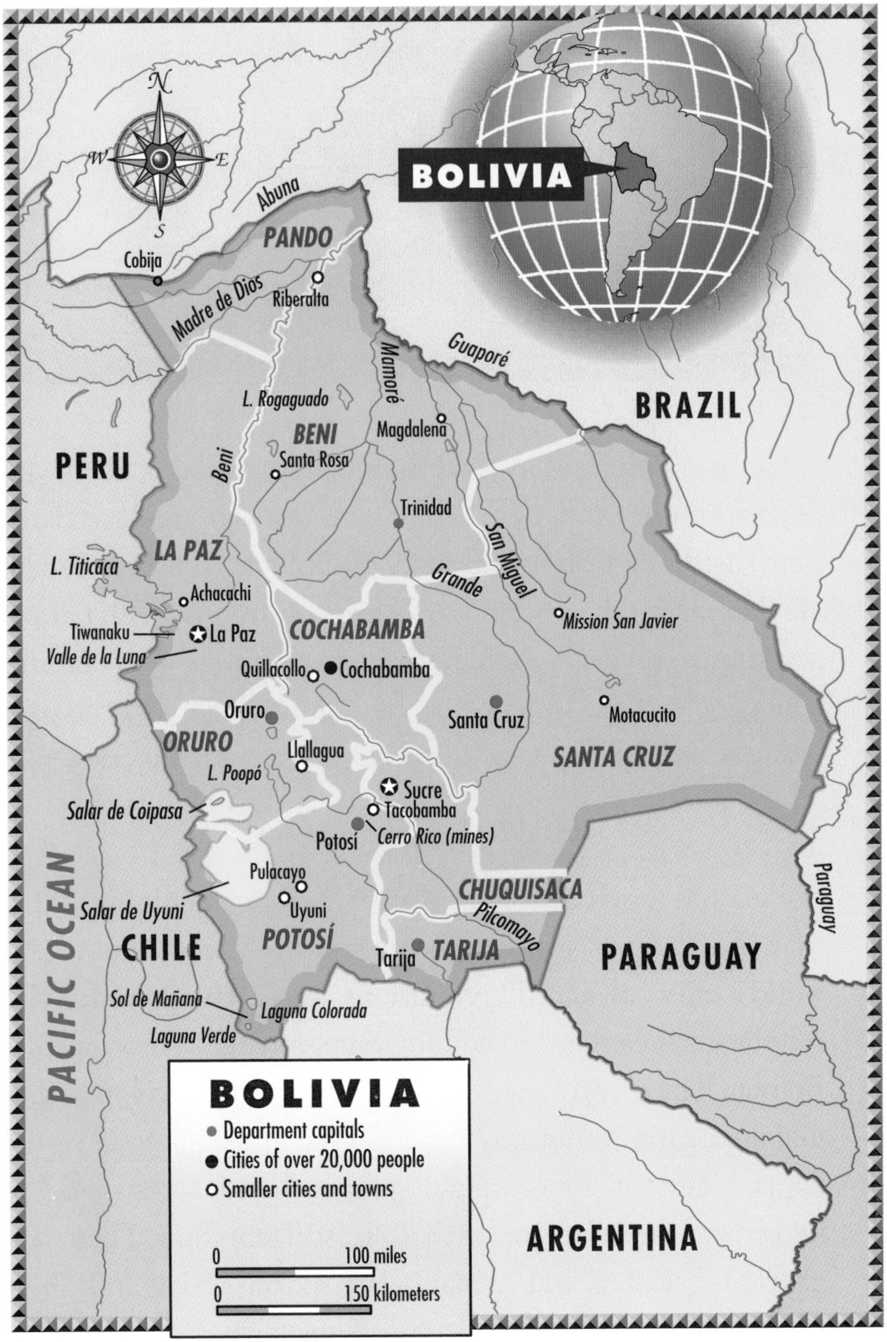

Geopolitical map of Bolivia

BOLIVIA

PERU

BRAZIL

PANDO

Cobija

Abuna

Madre de Dios

Riberalta

L. Rogaguado

BENI

Santa Rosa

Magdalena

Mamoré

Guaporé

Trinidad

San Miguel

LA PAZ

L. Titicaca

Achacachi

Tiwanaku — ✪ La Paz

Valle de la Luna

Quillacollo

COCHABAMBA

Cochabamba

Grande

Mission San Javier

Oruro

ORURO

Llallagua

L. Poopó

Santa Cruz

Motacucito

SANTA CRUZ

Salar de Coipasa

✪ Sucre

Tacobamba

Potosí

Cerro Rico (mines)

Pulacayo

Salar de Uyuni

Uyuni

CHUQUISACA

Pilcomayo

Paraguay

PACIFIC OCEAN

CHILE

POTOSÍ

Tarija

TARIJA

PARAGUAY

Sol de Mañana

Laguna Colorada

Laguna Verde

BOLIVIA
- Department capitals
- Cities of over 20,000 people
- Smaller cities and towns

0   100 miles
0   150 kilometers

ARGENTINA

A timber yard in the Oriente

An ancient stone carving at Tiwanaku

Bolivia's future is in the Oriente. The region is alive with opportunities. Santa Cruz de la Sierra (known simply as Santa Cruz) is the fastest-growing city in Bolivia. Young Bolivians are flocking to the lowlands to seek their fortune. Oil, natural gas, timber, soybeans, cattle, and manufacturing are booming. The people of the Oriente are less conservative and the pace of life is faster. The music is upbeat and the food is zesty.

Challenges

Bolivia has a rich history of Native American cultures. More than 2,000 years ago, Tiwanaku was the site of one of the world's most advanced civilizations. Later, the powerful and intelligent Inca ruled an empire that stretched across much of Bolivia. These early South American natives developed natural medicines, performed brain surgery, and domesticated the llama. They cut stones weighing more than 100 tons (90,720 kilograms), and built walls that are still standing. Their languages—Quechua and Aymara—are spoken widely in Bolivia today. However, the American Indians have not received an equal share of Bolivia's resources. In general, they have less land, less wealth, and less education. Opportunities for the native people need to be increased.

Major improvements in the transportation networks are crucial. Although Bolivia has more than 33,035 miles (53,163 kilometers) of highways, only 1,989 miles (3,200 km) were paved in 1995. During the rainy season, bridges wash away and landslides close highways in the mountains. Potholes and washboard surfaces turn roads into obstacle courses. These conditions are hard on vehicles, so trips may take three to four times as long as they would on good roads. The Bolivian government is working hard to finance major highway-improvement programs.

There are also environmental challenges. Bolivia recently signed a major international agreement to protect its rain forests. National parks and reserves are being expanded to protect endangered species. Mining companies are being challenged to clean up dangerous sites that contribute to air and water pollution.

Although Bolivia has many natural resources, it does not have great wealth. The country needs foreign investments to develop its economy. Additional funds from the World Bank, the International Monetary Fund, and the Inter-American Development Bank are also badly needed. The citizens of Bolivia have worked hard to provide a stable investment climate. Democracy is thriving. Capitalism and a market economy are flourishing. Bolivians are honest, hardworking people. They are eager to move forward and let the rest of the world know that Bolivia is a land of opportunity.

A Land of Contrasts

B OLIVIA'S IRREGULAR LAND BOUNDARIES FIT INTO CENTRAL South America like the pieces of a jigsaw puzzle. It is the fifth-largest country on the continent. Bolivia's landscape ranges from broad, flat plains to breathtaking mountain peaks. Temperatures may reach 115° Fahrenheit (46° Celsius) or fall to -60°F (-51°C). The nation has lush tropical forests as well as huge, barren plateaus. Bolivia has one of the most diverse landscapes in the world.

Opposite: **Lake Titicaca is the highest navigable lake in the world.**

Landlocked

Bolivia is spread over 424,165 square miles (1,098,587 sq km) of territory—about the same size as the combined area of Texas and California. The country shares almost 4,191 miles (6,743 km) of borders with its neighbors. Its northern and eastern neighbor is Brazil with more than one-half of the total border length (2,113 miles; 3,400 km). On the west, Peru (559 miles; 900 km) and Chile (535 miles; 861 km) block Bolivia's access to the Pacific Ocean. In the south, Argentina (517 miles; 832 km) and Paraguay (466 miles; 750 km) stand between Bolivia and the Atlantic Ocean. Bolivia has no direct access to the sea.

Bolivia has three major physical regions. The first region, the Andean Highlands, blankets the western third of the country. Here, a broad plateau forming Bolivia's highlands separates two major ranges of the Andes Mountains.

The second region, the Yungas, covers the eastern slopes of the Andes. This area consists of deep valleys with lush, green vegetation. The largest region is the Oriente, a vast lowland in northern and eastern Bolivia. It is covered by rain forests and grasslands in the north and east and by scrub forests in the south.

Farmland in the Yungas

Bolivia's Geographical Features

Highest Elevation: Mount Sajama, 21,463 feet (6,542 meters) above sea level

Lowest Elevation: Southeastern border with Paraguay, 300 feet (91 meters) above sea level

Highest Temperature: 115°F (46°C) in the Chaco

Lowest Temperature: -60°F (-51°C) in the Andes

Longest River: Mamoré, 1,242 miles (1,998 kilometers)

Highest Navigable Lake in the World: Lake Titicaca, 12,507 feet (3,812 meters) above sea level

South America's Deepest Lake: Lake Titicaca, 1,499 feet (457 meters) deep

World's Largest Salt Pan: Salar de Uyuni, 4,674 square miles (12,000 square kilometers)

World's Highest Capital City: La Paz, 12,001 feet (3,658 meters) above sea level

The Highlands

The Andes, which serve as the backbone of South America, split into two mountain ranges in western Bolivia. Running parallel with the border of Chile is the western range—the Cordillera Occidental. Many of the peaks here are volcanic, and several reach elevations of between 15,000 and 20,000 feet

(4,572 and 6,096 m). Mount Sajama, at 21,463 feet (6,542 m), is Bolivia's highest mountain. It is bitterly cold at these elevations and winds in excess of 80 miles (129 km) per hour frequently make conditions extremely harsh. Very few people live in these high mountains.

The eastern range, or Cordillera Oriental, is a series of individual ranges with local names. These mountain ranges begin north of Lake Titicaca and run in a southeasterly direction toward Paraguay. The ranges then turn sharply to the southwest and into Argentina.

These ranges provide some of the most dramatic scenery in Bolivia. Many of their summits are permanently snowcapped. The glaciers have carved steep, rugged canyons. Melting snow sends water cascading through cataracts over waterfalls, creating some of the most challenging whitewater rafting on the continent. The Indians believe that spirits live in the mountains and many people offer them gifts in exchange for protection.

Rolling hills, valleys, and broad basins dot the landscape in the southern portion of the Cordillera Oriental. Except for the summer rainy season (December to March), this region has the country's best climate with warm, sunny days and cool, refreshing nights. The soil is deep and fertile here, and fruits and vegetables thrive.

These highland valleys are the second most populated region in Bolivia, after the La Paz–Lake Titicaca area. The Spanish conquistadores fell in love with the climate and established a number of cities. Cochabamba, Sucre, Tarija, and Potosí were all Spanish colonial sites. Only Potosí was in

the high mountains, where temperatures were much colder because of altitude.

The Spanish established the city of Cochabamba in the Cordillera Oriental.

The Altiplano

In between the mountain ranges lies the vast Altiplano. This plateau is located mostly above 12,000 feet (3,658 m), and only the northern portion is densely populated. The soils are thin, the vegetation sparse, and the climate harsh. Nights are cold, frost is common, and roaring winds blast across the bleak landscape.

Valley of the Moon

A truly lunar landscape exists in a valley on the outskirts of La Paz in the *Valle de la Luna* (Valley of the Moon). Here, the forces of nature have cut through massive layers of clay to create a maze of miniature canyons and cathedral-like spires.

Life is hard for the highland Indians. In rural villages, most homes have neither electricity, nor running water or indoor plumbing. The farmers scratch out a living raising potatoes, beans, and *quinoa* (a high-protein cereal). Sheep, llama, and alpaca provide wool for clothing and meat. Moving south across the plateau, the population becomes sparser. Rainfall decreases and bodies of water such as Lake Poopó are salty. In the far southwestern corner of Bolivia, the landscape has an eerie, other-worldly appearance.

Adobe farm buildings in the Altiplano

Salar de Uyuni

Salar de Uyuni is the largest salt pan in the world. It covers 4,674 square miles (12,000 sq km), an area almost as large as the state of Connecticut. A salt pan is an accumulation of salt on the floor of a desert basin. Salar de Uyuni is estimated to contain more than 10 billion tons (9,072 billion kg) of fine salt. A few local *campesinos* (Indian farmers) gather small amounts of salt using a pickax and shovel.

An isolated volcanic island lies in the middle of the salt pan, 50 miles (80 km) from the shoreline. On the island, a spectacular stand of cactus grows 40 feet (12 m) tall. A stranded colony of *viscachas*, long-tailed rodents related to chinchillas, also live there.

A few miles from the edge of the salt pan stand two unusual hotels. Each hotel is made of more than 60,000 blocks of salt. The floors and walls—and even the beds, chairs, and tables—are made of salt. Workers using chain saws cut the blocks of salt from the surface of the salt pan.

Guests of the hotels awaken early to watch the sun rise over the distant mountains. Seeing the sun's rays reflect off the white salt surface is like standing on a polar icecap.

South of the Salar de Uyuni lie two spectacular lakes. The waters of Laguna Colorado are fiery red. It is the home of the rare James' flamingos. Laguna Verde is a beautiful blue-green lake located above 16,400 feet (5,000 m). The land between the lakes creates visions of hell. At Sol de Mañana, a geyser, bubbling mud pools, and vents belch stinky sulfurous gases into the fresh air.

Laguna Verde

The Yungas

On the eastern side of the Andes, nature has carved a magical environment. Deep valleys are covered with plush, green vegetation. This is the Yungas.

A cloud forest lies at the higher elevations. Raindrops can be seen moving horizontally as the clouds slip silently through the trees. Mosses and ferns cover the trees and forest floor. Droplets of water fall into crystal-clear pools and then trickle into small streams bound for the Amazon.

As the streams pick up speed, they become churning cascades of water. Rainbows appear as the sun's rays penetrate the mist of numerous waterfalls. An abundance of wildlife can be observed in this rich natural environment.

The rich natural environment of the Yungas

The Oriente covers two-thirds of Bolivia's land area. The tropical lowlands are a vast area of plains containing two major basins. In the north and east, many rivers drain into the Upper Amazon Basin. Large expanses of savanna grasslands intersect thick tropical rain forests along the rivers.

A port on the Mamoré River

Most of Bolivia's major rivers are found in the northeastern Oriente. The Madre de Dios, Beni, Mamoré, San Miguel, and Guapore carry billions of gallons of water to the Amazon each day. The rivers provide the major means of transportation in this region of Bolivia.

Southern and southeastern Bolivia are a part of the Paraná/Paraguay Basin. The Pilcomayo River is the longest tributary of the Paraguay River. The Pilcomayo is the major river of southeastern Bolivia. Its waters flow into the Paraguay River and eventually enter the Atlantic Ocean at the Río de la Plata.

In the far south of Bolivia's tropical lowlands, the plains become a part of the Gran Chaco. In this hot, dry, and dusty region, the vegetation consists of thorny scrub forestland with cactus and coarse grasses—a perfect home for the many poisonous snakes, scorpions, and biting insects. Local residents say that "everything in the Chaco either bites, stings, scratches, or pokes you."

Looking at Bolivia's Cities

Standing only 1,434 feet (437 m) above sea level, Santa Cruz is the gateway to Bolivia's rapidly developing Oriente. With a population of more than 950,000, it is the most progressive and wealthiest city in Bolivia. Santa Cruz is the center of the oil and natural gas industry, and has the best international airport in the country. Food-processing plants are scattered throughout the industrial manufacturing zone. The city was laid out by innovative planners in a series of concentric rings. Each ring has its center at the same point. Each ring has a separate function, such as a commercial zone, a residential zone, and an industrial zone. The residents, who call themselves *Cambas*, are noted for their warmth and good humor.

Founded in 1574, Cochabamba is Bolivia's third-largest city, with almost 580,000 people. It sits in a fertile, green valley 8,392 feet (2,558 m) above sea level. Cochabamba's citizens claim that their city has the world's most perfect climate. It is Bolivia's largest market town.

Trinidad is Bolivia's largest city in the Amazon lowlands, with a population of about 80,000. This cattle-marketing town is located along the banks of the Mamoré River. Fresh fish, such as surubí and pacú, are caught in the river and served in local restaurants. Motorcycles and mopeds are the major means of transportation here. Motorcycles and mopeds are even used as taxis!

A Reversal of Seasons

Sandwiched between 10 degrees and 23 degrees south latitude, Bolivia is a tropical country. In the Southern Hemisphere, the seasons are the opposite of those in the United States and Canada. So in Bolivia, summer arrives in December and winter begins in June.

Temperatures throughout the year are remarkably consistent across Bolivia. Altitude has a greater impact on temperatures than latitude has. Average annual temperatures in the lowlands are near 80°F (27°C). However, the average annual temperature in the highlands is only 47°F (8°C). The temperature may vary a lot in a single day. For example, it is not uncommon in La Paz to have the temperature change by 50°F (27.5°C) in one day. On the Altiplano, residents say the four seasons occur each day instead of each year: the cold nights are winter, mild mornings are spring, the heat of midday represents summer, and the cool evenings are autumn. People there dress in layers. As the daytime temperature warms, they peel off their clothing layer by layer.

Rain and Drought

Rainfall across Bolivia is seasonally consistent. Most of the country experiences the same wet and dry seasons. Most rain falls in summer between December and March. In winter, from May to September, little rain falls—except in the Yungas and tropical lowlands. These areas may have rain any day of the year.

The total rainfall decreases from northeastern Bolivia to the southwest. The tropical lowlands generally get at least

60 inches (152 centimeters) of rain each year. In the wet season, the sky opens and torrents of rain flood the land. Roads turn to mud and soon become impassable. However, this seasonal flooding is necessary for the survival of the rain forest.

Farther south in the Chaco, rainfall decreases to a yearly average of 20 inches (51 cm). Drought is a constant threat in this region. Most of the year, hot winds deposit a layer of dust on the vegetation. When it finally does rain, the dust changes to mud.

Most of the Altiplano receives 20 to 25 inches (50 to 64 cm) of rain annually. The exception is the southwestern corner near Chile. Here, part of the world's driest desert, the Atacama, has truly arid conditions. Annual rainfall is often less than 10 inches (25 cm). In some years, the parched environment gets less than 5 inches (13 cm).

Drought is a threat to the dry grasslands of the Chaco.

Treasures of Nature

B OLIVIA HAS BEEN DESCRIBED AS ONE HUGE WILDLIFE park. The country ranks sixth in the world in the number of species of plants and animals found within its borders. Much of this diversity is the result of the nation's geography. The ecosystems of the Andes and Altiplano are different from those of the Yungas. The rain forests of the tropical lowlands have the greatest abundance of plant and animal species. And in the Chaco, scientists are still discovering new species.

Opposite: **Tourists trekking in the Yungas**

A Harsh Environment

On the Altiplano, the weather is cold, dry, and windy. Each year, temperatures fall below freezing on 110 to 200 nights. These conditions limit the number of biological species that can live there.

A quenua tree

Natural vegetation is sparse. Clumps of tough grass called *ichu* cover the highland meadows. Short, rugged thola bushes occasionally appear. Only the quenua tree can grow there. The quenua is the only native tree species that grows above 9,843 feet (3,000 m) in the Andean area. In fact, the quenua has been known to grow at elevations above 17,388 feet (5,300 m). A virgin stand of quenua trees grows at the base of Mount Sajama, Bolivia's highest

peak. Bolivians claim it is the highest forest in the world. The conditions on the Altiplano also limit the kinds of crops that farmers can grow. But the highland Indians have been successful in raising two important plants—the potato and the quinoa.

More than 200 different varieties of potatoes are grown in Bolivia. Since prehistoric times, the potato has been the main source of food in the highlands. Today, the average Bolivian eats 286 pounds (129 kg) of potatoes each year.

Quinoa growing in the Andes

In pre-Columbian times, quinoa was the major source of protein for Inca armies. Quinoa produces a small, milletlike seed high in protein. The plant can survive in both drought and frost. Quinoa is frequently grown above the tree line. Its hanging seeds form a thick, tangled stalk. Frequently, highland women roast quinoa over an open fire.

The number of animal species in the highlands is small compared with the lowlands but the environment has a few animals. Elusive Andean mountain cats prowl the slopes of the mountains while rodents scurry into holes and cracks on the rocky surface. And more than 150 different species of birds live there, too.

Relatives of the Camel

Four descendants of the camel family, called camelids, live in Bolivia's highlands. They are the llama, the alpaca, the guanaco, and the vicuña. The llama and alpaca have been domesticated for 4,000 to 5,000 years. The guanaco and vicuña are still wild animals.

These camelids are perfectly suited for the Altiplano's sensitive environment. They nibble on grasses rather than pulling them up by the roots. Their digestive system is very efficient. As a result, several camelids require less grass than one horse. They are not as likely to damage natural grasses by overgrazing. Camelids consume very little water, which may be in short supply in the region.

Domesticated llamas and alpacas have always been important to the highland Indians. The llama are used to carry products in trade and its wool is used to make clothing. The wool fiber is hollow, so it is very light. It is the perfect material to protect against the bitterly cold winds of the Altiplano. Llama meat can be eaten fresh or dried to produce *chorqui*. Chorqui, the origin of the English word *jerky*, is a native Quechua word. Finally, llama dung is used for fuel or fertilizer. The Alpacas were domesticated primarily for their wool.

The guanaco and vicuña are smaller animals and were never tamed. However, they were nearly hunted into extinction for their wool. This is especially true of the vicuña. The vicuña is now an endangered species and is vigorously protected. Only about 27,000 vicuñas are living today,

Indians keep alpacas for their wool.

The National Bird

The Andean condor is Bolivia's national bird. It is featured in a prominent position on the country's national emblem. Standing more than 4 feet (122 cm) high, the condor has a wingspan of up to 10 feet (3 m). With an average weight of 20 to 25 pounds (9 to 11 kg), it is the world's heaviest bird of prey.

A howler monkey

most of them in Bolivia. The vicuña produces about 4 ounces (113 grams) of wool a year. The fiber is so fine that it feels as if a cloud has passed across your cheek when you hold it next to your face. During the Inca era, the fleece was so valuable that only royalty were allowed to wear it.

Exotic Landscapes

Descending from Bolivia's highlands into the eastern lowlands is an exhilarating ecological experience. The drab colors of the Altiplano are replaced by the lush, rich greens of the Yungas. Stunted shrubs and bushes change to towering trees draped with vines. Flowering plants produce colorful blossoms of orange, yellow, and red. Chattering monkeys swing from tree to tree. Brightly colored birds flit through the branches singing and calling. The Yungas is alive with activity.

Situated on the eastern slopes of the Andes, the Yungas benefits from its location. The tropical sun raises temperatures above 80°F (27°C) daily. Gentle trade winds off the Atlantic Ocean bring warm, moist air and ample rain throughout the year. The region is hot and humid.

One of the best ways to experience the Yungas is to walk through it. Trekking is a popular tourist activity in the region. Hikers from around the world come to Bolivia to follow the ancient Inca trails. These hikers may see multicolored butterflies and snakes, soaring eagles, and several endangered species.

Macaws and other brightly colored birds live in the Yungas.

Good and Evil

One of the most interesting plants in the Yungas is the coca plant. It thrives under the same conditions as the coffee plant—rich soils and tropical climates. The coca plant prefers the slightly cooler temperatures found on slopes between 1,500 and 4,000 feet (457 and 1,219 m) high. It is one of the oldest crops grown in South America.

Andean people have used the leaf of the coca plant for centuries, mainly as a stimulant and a medicine. The leaf contains a natural narcotic substance.

The Indians of Bolivia either brew a tea, coca maté, or chew the leaf like tobacco. However,

Coca growing on a mountain slope

instead of spitting out the juice produced from chewing the leaf, they swallow it. Coca is most commonly used in the highlands, where it reduces the effects of *soroche* (altitude sickness). Working and living in the oxygen-deficient air can lead to fatigue, dizziness, headaches, and an upset stomach. The coca leaf relieves these symptoms and produces a soothing effect.

The coca plant was considered a sacred plant by the Inca. Inca *shamans*, or healers, used the coca leaf to make an anesthetic used in surgery. It was also used to treat ulcers, rheumatism, asthma, and eye infections. In the United States, Thomas Edison, the great American inventor, and President Ulysses Grant were treated with medicines made from coca.

The coca plant has a dark side, however. It is now part of an illegal drug trade valued at billions of dollars. The extract of the coca leaf is used to produce cocaine, a harmful narcotic drug. Many people have become addicted to cocaine and ruined their lives.

The government of Bolivia is working hard to get rid of coca plants used for drugs. But the task is difficult. Poor Bolivian farmers can make more money growing coca plants than any other crop. In the United States, some people blame Bolivia for the U.S. drug problem but Americans share the blame at least equally. If people in the United States and other nations did not create a demand for cocaine, Bolivians would not grow it.

Protecting Nature's Gifts

The tropical lowlands of Bolivia's Oriente provide the country's richest diversity of plant and animal life. For many years, this region was isolated and sparsely populated. Even today, almost half of its original forests are still standing. These forests and the adjoining grasslands provide a home for many species that do not exist anywhere else on our planet.

Bolivians are aware of the unique environment they call home. As a result, they have created ten national parks and eight protected areas covering thousands of square miles. The government is also reviewing six additional sites for protected area status.

Much of Bolivia's environmental awareness is the result of one man's work. Dr. Noel Kempff, a noted Bolivian biologist, was also the country's most famous environmentalist. Kempff traveled to the most remote corners of Bolivia to study the country's ecosystems. He studied the negative impact of logging and agriculture on natural habitats, and reported his findings to the government. He tirelessly promoted laws that would protect Bolivia's natural treasures. He found and collected species for the country's most notable zoo in Santa Cruz.

On September 5, 1986, Kempff was murdered by drug smugglers while conducting research in the jungle. The Bolivian government named its largest and most famous national park, Noel Kempff Mercado National Park, in his memory.

National Parks and Reserves

■ National Park   ■ National Reserve

The Rain Forests

The tropical rain forests of Bolivia run into the Amazon Basin of neighboring Brazil. Two-thirds of the world's known plant species

Amazing Diversity

Noel Kempff Mercado National Park is approximately the same size as the state of Massachusetts. Scientists have registered an amazing diversity of flora and fauna in the park, including more than 4,000 species of plants, 625 species of birds, 246 species of fish, 139 species of mammals, 74 species of reptiles, and 62 species of amphibians.

Capybaras are the world's largest rodents.

are found in these rain forests. Still more plant species, which may hold the cure for crippling or fatal diseases, remain undiscovered. This is only one reason why the destruction of any rain forest is not in the best interests of humans.

In Bolivia, the rain forests also provide a natural habitat for plants and animals that cannot survive elsewhere. Freshwater river dolphins and giant otters play in the swirling rivers. Giant anteaters, capybaras (the world's largest rodents), and the rare maned wolf prowl the forest floor. In the trees overhead, monkeys scamper from branch to branch. A sudden noise sends hundreds of brightly colored parrots screeching through the trees.

Disappearing Grasslands

The grasslands of the lowlands are changing rapidly. Many of the wild animals are feeling the pressure of human activity. Millions of farm animals are now being raised on the lowland grasses in Beni, Pando, and Santa Cruz Departments (political subdivisions).

Natural grasses are being plowed under to grow crops. The landscape is checkered with fields of soybeans, corn, and sorghum. The use of chemicals for fertilizer, pesticides, and herbicides also poses a threat to the natural environment. Eroded soil materials clog the streams and rivers with silt.

The Chaco

Plant and animal life in the Chaco region of southeastern Bolivia reflect the arid and semiarid environment. Many

A six-banded armadillo in the Chaco

plants have xerophytic characteristics. Xerophyte plants can survive with limited rainfall. They have deep taproots that enable them to reach underground water. They have small leaves that prevent the loss of water through giving off water vapor. They have thorns and spikes that keep animals away.

The animals that live in the Chaco have also adjusted to the environment. Their hides are tough and their hair is coarse. Peccaries, which are related to pigs, grunt and root on the floor of the scrub forest. The weak-sighted armadillo, protected by its tanklike shell, claws for grubs and insects. Jaguars hunt relentlessly for unsuspecting prey while poachers hunt the jaguar for its beautiful fur.

Bolivia has been blessed with a wonderful diversity of plants and animals. The country also has been given a responsibility to protect its natural gifts. Balancing the development of the country's economy with protection of its environment is a big challenge for the citizens of Bolivia.

The Spectacled Bear

The rare spectacled bear can be found in Amboró National Park. The light-colored fur around its eyes makes it look like it is wearing glasses, or spectacles. It is the only species of bear in South America. Scientists estimate its population at under 2,000. The bear's diet is 95 percent vegetarian. It does not hibernate because its food sources are available throughout the year.

Reflections from the Past

BOLIVIA'S EARLY HISTORY IS CLOUDED WITH MANY unanswered questions. When did humans first arrive? Where did they come from? How did they get to Bolivia?

Slowly but surely, modern scholars are beginning to answer these questions. Many scientists believe that the first humans arrived in Bolivia approximately 10,000 to 12,000 years ago. They think the early inhabitants came from Asia to North America over a land bridge across the Bering Strait. Gradually, they moved southward through North America, Central America, and into South America.

The early residents lived simple but difficult lives. They were hunters and gatherers who survived by using what nature provided. Eventually, they began to band together into small communities. Over time, their settlements became permanent. They grew native plants and domesticated animals. The potato became a staple in their diet. Llamas and alpacas were tamed to serve as beasts of burden and to provide meat, clothing, fuel, and fertilizer.

Opposite: **The Wall of Faces at Tiwanaku**

A Grand Civilization

As early as 1600 B.C., a highly civilized community began to develop near Lake Titicaca at a site called Tiwanaku. The Tiwanakan culture reached its peak between A.D. 400 and 900. By A.D. 1000, the site was abandoned, and by 1200 the civilization had disappeared.

Overgrown foundations and walls are still visible today at Tiwanaku.

A feline god from Tiwanaku

The ruins of the great city of Tiwanaku reflect the genius of its inhabitants. At one time, the city covered 2.3 square miles (6 sq km). An estimated 20,000 to 50,000 people lived in and around the city amid pyramids, palaces, and elaborate sculptures carved from stone. The rulers of Tiwanaku controlled a vast empire reaching from Peru to Argentina and from the Pacific Ocean to the eastern slopes of the Andes.

The Tiwanakans were expert architects and builders. They built stone structures that represented the heavens, the earth, and the underworld. They cut blocks of stone weighing more than 100 tons (90,720 kg) from an ancient volcano near Copacabana. They floated these blocks across Lake Titicaca on wooden rafts. Other gigantic pieces of sandstone were cut from nearby mountains.

Once the huge slabs of rock reached Tiwanaku, craftsmen polished the pieces. Each slab was then locked in place with copper pins or brackets. Some of the walls are still standing after more than 1,000 years.

The Tiwanakans were also skilled astronomers. They studied the stars and the apparent movement of the sun across the sky. They understood the solstice and the equinox. The Sun Gate, a massive stone weighing 10 tons (9,072 kg), served as an opening to a temple. Originally, the entire stone was covered with gold. Visitors to Tiwanaku were dazzled by the reflection of the sun off the Sun Gate.

A subterranean structure, which represented the underworld, still contains some curious carvings. Placed in the walls of the complex are facial images of extraterrestrial beings. Some have faces identical to modern drawings of space aliens. Others have heads with large craniums or brain enclosures. The origin of these images remains a great mystery.

The Sun Gate

An Agricultural Mystery

For many years, scientists were puzzled by the existence of this prosperous civilization on the barren Altiplano. Its existence had been hidden for over 1,000 years. Then, when scholars studied aerial photographs of the site, a series of ridges and depressions were visible.

Closer investigation uncovered an agricultural system that stunned observers. The Tiwanakans were brilliant hydrologists—experts on the properties of water. They invented the construction of raised fields. The fields were 656 feet (200 m) long and 50 feet (15 m) wide.

The bases of the raised fields were made of cobblestones for stability. Then, a thin layer of clay was used to retain water. Three distinct layers of gravel on top of the clay provided drainage. The top layer was a thick, rich layer of organic topsoil.

In between the ridges, canals covered about 30 percent of the field surface. They carried water for irrigation. At night, the water released the heat it had absorbed from the sun. The released heat prevented frost damage.

The fields and canals covered almost 30,000 acres (12,146 hectares) of the Altiplano. Food production from these fields supported a population of up to 50,000, and may have provided a surplus for export.

The End

Around A.D. 1000, the fields and the great city were abandoned. When the Spanish arrived and saw Tiwanaku, they questioned the local natives about its origin. The natives told the Spanish that they did not know who had lived there. There were no records.

Recent studies of deposits along the shores of Lake Titicaca have revealed new evidence. Apparently, a drought that lasted several decades hit the area. Without water in the canals, the crops would have failed. Malnutrition and starvation forced the Tiwanakans to abandon their fabulous city.

From 1200 to 1438, the Bolivian highlands were ruled by the Kollas. The Kollas were a brutal tribe believed to have come from southern Peru. They did not establish a society equal to the Tiwanakan civilization.

The Inca Empire

In the 1430s, the powerful Inca swept across the western part of Bolivia. The highland Indians became a part of a vast empire ruled from Cuzco, Peru. Once a region was taken over, its people were expected to be loyal to the Inca leader.

The Inca people believed that their leader was the son of the sun, and they viewed him as a god. He lived a life of luxury. His palaces were decorated in gold and silver, and he wore robes made of bat fur and hummingbird wings. These robes were worn only once and then discarded.

The Inca ruled Bolivia as a welfare state. Food, clothing, and shelter were provided for the elderly and needy. All healthy citizens were expected to work a certain number of days each year for the state. The punishment for laziness was death.

Ruins of an Inca observatory
at Lake Titicaca

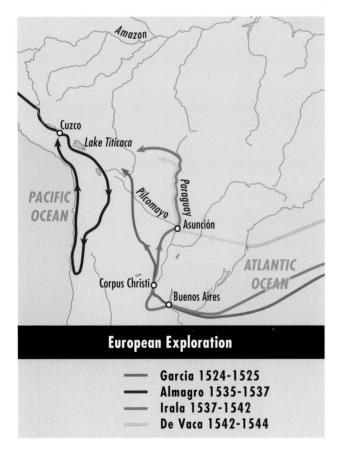

European Exploration

— Garcia 1524-1525
— Almagro 1535-1537
— Irala 1537-1542
— De Vaca 1542-1544

The Inca also taught the conquered people their Inca religion and language. The Inca spoke a language called Quechua, and worshiped the sun. In Bolivia, the Inca made a rare exception. They did not require their Bolivian subjects living near Lake Titicaca to speak Quechua. They allowed them to continue to speak Aymara, the language of Tiwanaku. Legend says that the Inca were in awe of the great ruins of Tiwanaku. Out of respect for the Tiwanakan culture, Aymara remained an important language.

Life under the Inca required hard work. Yet basic needs were met and the empire prospered. But the Inca would rule highland Bolivia for only a century.

Horses, Guns, and Disaster

In 1529, Inca messengers sent reports of a troubling nature to Cuzco. Bearded men dressed in silver suits were spotted on floating houses in the ocean. The Spanish had arrived along the coast of Peru. Their arrival in Peru changed Bolivia's history dramatically.

In 1532, Spanish explorer Francisco Pizarro moved inland searching for gold and silver. He soon encountered Atahualpa, son of Huayna Capac, the last great Inca chief. Pizarro sent an officer to invite Atahualpa to supper. Atahualpa scoffed at the invitation and prepared to slaughter the Spaniards the next day.

The Spaniards were greatly outnumbered. Pizarro had 62 mounted men and 102 foot soldiers. Atahualpa commanded nearly 50,000 warriors. The Spaniards plotted a secret attack. They would

Francisco Pizarro

Atahualpa being carried on his throne

lure Atahualpa and his men into a city square. The mounted men and foot soldiers would hide inside doorways surrounding the square.

At dusk on November 16, 1532, the Inca Empire came tumbling down. After Atahualpa and his warriors entered the square, a bugle sounded. Gunshots rang out. Horses pounded out of doorways, their steel shoes clanging on the cobblestone streets. The Inca, who had never seen horses, fled in terror. Spanish swords sliced their bodies. Lances pierced their backs. Hundreds were trampled to death. When the smoke and dust had settled, 7,000 Inca lay dead and Atahualpa was a prisoner. The Spanish colonial period in the Andes had begun.

Spaniards in Bolivia

In 1538, Gonzalo and Hernando Pizarro, Francisco Pizarro's brothers, arrived in Bolivia. They established a local administrative center at La Plata, later named Chuquisaca, and finally Sucre. A mining camp was also established at Porco. Local administrators were responsible to the Viceroyalty of Peru in Lima. For the next several years, only a few Spaniards came to Bolivia. That changed suddenly after 1544, when an Indian peasant named Diego Huallpa made a remarkable discovery—a rich silver deposit.

Potosí, City of Silver

Word of the discovery of silver filtered back to the Spanish. In 1545, four Spanish Army captains took possession of the mountain. They claimed it in the name of Charles V, Emperor

The city of Potosí was founded in 1545.

of Spain. Miners flocked to the mountain, which the Spanish renamed *Cerro Rico* (Rich Mountain). In 1545, the city of Potosí was founded at the base of Cerro Rico.

In the first thirty years of mining, $1.5 billion worth of silver was sent to the king of Spain. An equal amount was hidden and kept by local officials. Potosí became one of the wealthiest cities in the world. By 1650, its population had grown to 160,000. It was the largest city in the Western Hemisphere, larger than Madrid, Paris, or London. Wealthy miners built churches with gold and silver altars.

For more than 200 years, the silver of Cerro Rico financed the extravagance

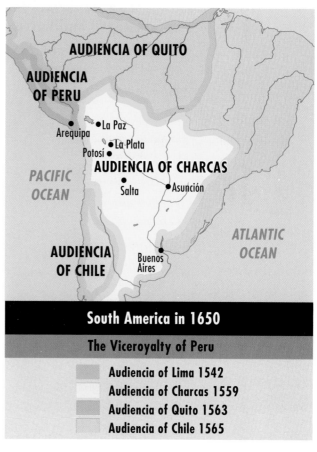

AUDIENCIA OF QUITO

AUDIENCIA OF PERU

PACIFIC OCEAN

Arequipa • •La Paz
Potosí • •La Plata
AUDIENCIA OF CHARCAS
Salta • •Asunción

AUDIENCIA OF CHILE
Buenos Aires •

ATLANTIC OCEAN

South America in 1650

The Viceroyalty of Peru

Audiencia of Lima 1542
Audiencia of Charcas 1559
Audiencia of Quito 1563
Audiencia of Chile 1565

of the Spanish Crown. Their wealth was squandered on European wars and lavish lifestyles. The cost to the native people was horrible.

Forced to labor under inhuman conditions in the mines, the Indians and the imported African slaves died like flies. Many got pneumonia from working in the cold, damp mine-shafts. Others died from inhaling mercury fumes at the smelters. Daily accidents killed still more. It has been said that a bridge of silver could have been built from Potosí to Madrid with the ore of Cerro Rico. Likewise, a bridge of bones could have been built with the bodies of the dead miners. An estimated 8 million workers died over three centuries under forced labor at Cerro Rico.

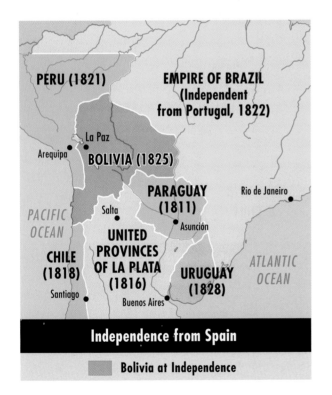

Independence from Spain

Bolivia at Independence

The Spanish colonial period was marked by mining and agricultural development. Large expanses of land were taken from the indigenous people. Huge estates were established. The natives were forced to work the land by their Spanish overlords. This period of history provided little benefit for the native people.

Independence from Spain

In Europe, conditions were changing rapidly. The Napoleonic Wars had weakened the authority of the Spanish Crown. The French Revolution and U.S. Declaration of Independence sparked discussions of independence for Bolivia.

In 1809, Bolivia proclaimed its independence from Spain. Sixteen years of struggle followed.

Simón Bolívar of Venezuela led the struggle. He sought independence for Venezuela, Colombia, Peru, Ecuador, and Bolivia. In Peru, Bolívar's lieutenant, Antonio José de Sucre defeated the Spanish at the Battle of Ayacucho in 1824. A year later, on August 6, 1825, Bolivia was declared a republic.

Casa de la Libertad in Sucre, where Bolivia's independence was declared

Simón Bolívar

The new republic chose Bolivia for its name in honor of Bolívar, "The Liberator." The citizens of Bolivia appointed Bolívar as its protector and first president. Bolívar served only a few months as president. In January 1826, Sucre was elected as the first constitutional president of Bolivia.

The creation of the republic did not bring stability to Bolivia, however. Between 1825 and 1981, there were 192 *coups d'état* (sudden changes of government). Over that 156-year period, change occurred once every ten months on average. Regional jealousy promoted a lack of unity, and the native people had no political, economic, or educational opportunities.

On many occasions, cruel military dictators led the nation. The most notorious was General Mariano Melgarejo Valencia. He had an ex-president, Isidoro Belzú Humérez, murdered in the presidential office. He squandered the nation's treasury on his mistress. He initiated the government's seizure and sale of the Indian communal land. In 1867, he foolishly ceded a large area of rubber-rich territory to Brazil. A recent newspaper survey ranking Bolivian leaders listed Melgarejo as Bolivia's worst president.

A Costly War

Chile, Bolivia's western neighbor, also took advantage of the country's internal problems. From 1879 to 1883, the two countries fought over rich nitrate deposits in Bolivia's western province. The conflict was called the War of the Pacific.

Bolivia lost the war and, with it, a large piece of territory including its rich nitrate deposits. It also lost its access to the Pacific Ocean and the port of Antofagasta. Bolivia was now a landlocked country. The war caused a deep scar in Bolivia's relations with Chile. More than a hundred years later, many Bolivians still resent the Chilean government.

The Tin Barons

In the late 1800s, an increase in silver prices brought some stability to Bolivia. This stability continued into the 1920s, when tin replaced silver as the major export. Bolivia soon became the world's number one exporter of tin. Simón Patiño, Carlos Aramayo, and Maurico Hochschild, who controlled the tin-mining industry, were listed among the wealthiest men in the world.

American Outlaws

In 1908, two of the most notorious outlaws from the United States died in Bolivia. Butch Cassidy and the Sundance Kid had traveled to Bolivia to rob mule trains carrying silver. They perished in a shoot-out with the Bolivian army near the dusty village of San Vicente.

A tin mine at Cerro Rico today

With their immense wealth, they controlled the politics of Bolivia. Politicians and lawyers were paid to protect their interests. But political stability came at a price. Miners and landless peasants were poorly paid and were not allowed to protest.

The Chaco War

Between 1932 and 1935, Bolivia fought a disastrous war against Paraguay. Known as the Chaco War, it cost Bolivia 50,000 to 60,000 men and hundreds of millions of dollars. In the end, Bolivia lost most of its vast Chaco territory. The country also lost significant reserves of oil and natural gas. In a little over a century, Bolivia had lost more than half of its territory to wars and ill-advised political decisions.

A Bolivian patrol in the Chaco War with Paraguay

Political Reform

The Chaco War did have a positive result though. It showed how poor the political and military leadership was, and it stirred feelings of nationalism among the native people. Eventually it led to major reforms.

The Nationalist Revolutionary Movement (*Movimiento Nacionalista Revolucionario*, or MNR) emerged as a major political party. In 1951, under the leadership of Víctor Paz Estenssoro, the MNR won the presidency. However, a military coup prevented Estenssoro from taking office. The voters were outraged. An armed revolt broke out, and the military was defeated. The 1952 Revolution succeeded in placing the elected president, Estenssoro, in office.

The revolution led to sweeping political reform. All Bolivian adults were granted the right to vote. Rural education was promoted. Indian lands were returned to their rightful owners. The tin mines were nationalized, breaking the political power of the tin barons.

Political Chaos

After twelve years of MNR rule, the country slipped back into chaos. A series of elected governments and military dictatorships followed. In 1966, General René Barrientos Ortuño was elected president, but his administration was plagued by labor unrest and strikes. In southeastern Bolivia, a left-wing guerrilla uprising was led by Ernesto "Ché" Guevara. Guevara had played a significant role in the Cuban revolution that brought Fidel Castro to power. Although Guevara had hoped

General Luis Garcia Meza

for the same results in Bolivia, his attempt was cut short when he was captured and killed in 1967.

In 1980, General Luis Garcia Meza took power in a ruthless and violent coup. He hired Klaus Barbie, a former Nazi and Gestapo chief, as his internal security adviser. In Europe, Barbie had been known as the "Butcher of Leon" for his role in killing thousands of Jews.

Barbie formed a paramilitary group, *Los Novios de la Muerte* (The Newlyweds of Death). With Garcia Meza's backing and money from cocaine traffickers, a reign of terror began in Bolivia. All opposition was repressed. Political opponents were arrested, tortured, or disappeared.

Finally, the country had seen enough. The military ousted Garcia Meza. New elections resulted in victory for Dr. Hernán Siles Zuazo. However, labor strikes, political unrest, and an astronomical inflation rate of more than 14,000 percent a year doomed the Zuazo presidency. He stepped down from the president's office a year early so that new elections could be held.

The Dawn of a New Era

In July 1985, Víctor Paz Estenssoro was elected to his third term as president. Paz Estenssoro moved quickly to improve conditions in Bolivia. He set up a program called the New Economic Policy (*Nueva Politicia Economica*, or NPE). Under this program, government budgets were frozen, price subsidies were eliminated, and thousands of state workers were laid off. Relations with the United States improved.

President Hugo Bánzer Suárez

Although many workers suffered, inflation was brought under control. Free-market policies cured the sick economy. Most remarkably, Paz Estenssoro was able to finish his term in office without a coup. Political stability had returned to Bolivia.

Since Paz Estenssoro completed his term in office, all elected presidents have served their full term. In June 1997, General Hugo Bánzer Suárez was elected president. He is continuing the policies of the past three administrations. New trade agreements have been negotiated, and development is encouraged, with environmental restraint. Bolivia is moving forward in the twenty-first century.

Governing the People

The citizens of Bolivia have experienced many different types of government. They have been a part of empires whose rulers considered themselves gods. They have been subjects of a foreign colonial power with few individual rights. The country has struggled with dictators and unstable leadership. All of these experiences have contributed to a commitment to build a strong democracy.

Opposite: **The National Congress in La Paz**

The Republic of Bolivia was recognized as an independent nation on August 6, 1825, and its first Constitution was approved in November 1826. The Constitution, which serves as a blueprint for how the country will be governed, has been changed many times. The last major change was in 1967, and modest reforms were made in 1994. The current Constitution divides the duties of the government into three branches—executive, legislative, and judicial.

The President's Guard

Executive Leadership

The executive branch of government is made up of the president, the vice president, and the cabinet. The president and vice president must be members of the same political party. They are elected by the people for a five-year term and are not eligible for

Dr. Víctor Paz Estenssoro

In 1983, thirty-two out of thirty-nine prominent Bolivians rated President Dr. Víctor Paz Estenssoro as one of Bolivia's best presidents. His service to his country was remarkable. In 1951, he won the presidential vote while living in exile in Argentina. The military's refusal to allow him to return to Bolivia led to the 1952 Revolution.

After the revolution, Paz Estenssoro served his first term as president from 1952 to 1956. He made difficult but necessary decisions regarding voting rights, land reform, education, and nationalization of the tin mines.

Paz Estenssoro was elected president a second time in 1960 and served until 1964. Between 1985 and 1989, he served his third term as president. When he was elected in 1985, Bolivia was facing a severe economic crisis. A rate of inflation of more than 14,000 percent had made Bolivia's money worthless. Social unrest and labor strikes paralyzed the nation. Exports were declining, and drug trafficking was out of control. President Paz Estenssoro once again provided the leadership that restored the economy and the nation's credibility.

immediate reelection after their five-year term. However, the Constitution allows them to seek election after being out of office for one term. If the president resigns or dies in office, the vice president becomes head of state until new elections are held. The president acts as both chief of state and head of the government.

As chief of state, the president is responsible for conducting foreign affairs. He also has the power to issue presidential decrees. His greatest power comes with the initiation of legislation through special messages to Congress.

The president is also responsible for the appointment of cabinet members, diplomatic representatives, archbishops, and bishops. The president makes these appointments from a panel of candidates submitted by the Senate. The cabinet helps the president run the executive branch of government. There are fourteen cabinet-level offices, including National Defense, Foreign Affairs, Justice, Labor, Finance, Health, Education, and Agriculture.

Congressional Representation

Bolivia's National Congress is made up of two separate groups that create legislation. One is the Senate, and the other is the Chamber of Deputies. The Senate has 27 members. Three senators are elected from each of nine political departments—political divisions of the country similar to states and provinces in the United States and Canada. The Chamber of Deputies has 130 members. In 1996, a constitutional amendment introduced direct elections by the people for 65 deputies. The remaining deputies are nominated by political party leaders.

The Bolivian Flag

The current flag of Bolivia was first used in 1851 and was officially adopted in 1888. It has three horizontal stripes of equal dimensions. The top stripe is red and represents the animal kingdom. The middle stripe is yellow and represents Bolivia's rich mineral resources; it displays Bolivia's coat of arms. The green stripe at the bottom of the flag represents vegetation.

The Chamber of Deputies in session

Bolivia's Political Divisions

Department	Capital	Area
Beni	Trinidad	82,457 sq mi (213,564 sq km)
Chuquisaca	Sucre	19,893 sq mi (51,523 sq km)
Cochabamba	Cochabamba	21,479 sq mi (55,631 sq km)
La Paz	La Paz	51,732 sq mi (133,986 sq km)
Oruro	Oruro	20,690 sq mi (53,587 sq km)
Pando	Cobija	24,644 sq mi (63,828 sq km)
Potosí	Potosí	45,644 sq mi (118,218 sq km)
Santa Cruz	Santa Cruz	143,097 sq mi (370,621 sq km)
Tarija	Tarija	14,526 sq mi (37,622, sq km)

Representatives to both houses of the National Congress are elected for five-year terms. The Congress meets for one session each year. The session lasts 90 working days but may be extended to 120 days. During each session, the Congress debates the pros and cons of new legislation. After debate, representatives vote on the proposed legislation.

Bolivia's Supreme Court is in Sucre.

The Judicial Process

The Supreme Court is the highest court in the land. Twelve justices sit on the bench of the Court. The Congress appoints them for a term of ten years. The responsibilities of the Court are divided into four chambers, with three justices in each chamber. Two chambers deal with civil law, one chamber deals with criminal cases, and the final chamber handles administrative, social, and mining cases.

There are also district courts in each of the country's nine departments. A district attorney is appointed for each departmental court. In addition, provincial and local courts try minor cases.

Regional Government

An individual called a prefect governs each department. Prefects are appointed by the president. They serve as the administrative, political, and military authority in their department. The prefect's role is similar to that of state and provincial governors in the United States and Canada.

NATIONAL GOVERNMENT OF BOLIVIA

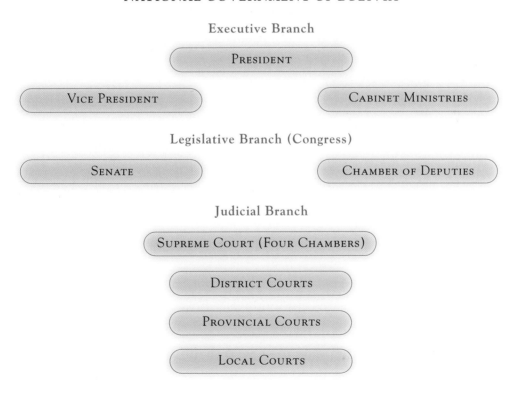

Executive Branch

PRESIDENT

VICE PRESIDENT   CABINET MINISTRIES

Legislative Branch (Congress)

SENATE   CHAMBER OF DEPUTIES

Judicial Branch

SUPREME COURT (FOUR CHAMBERS)

DISTRICT COURTS

PROVINCIAL COURTS

LOCAL COURTS

A candidate for mayor voting in the 1999 elections

Marking the Ballot

For many years, most Bolivian citizens were not allowed to vote in elections. Individuals who could not read and write were prohibited from voting. The 1952 Revolution changed voting restrictions. A government decree allowed anyone twenty-one years old or older to vote. In 1994, the voting age for married citizens was changed to eighteen. All eligible voters are required to vote in Bolivian elections.

There are fifteen major political parties in Bolivia. Some are liberal, some are moderate, and some are conservative.

Two Capitals

Bolivia is one of the few countries in the world with two capitals. The constitutional and legal capital is Sucre. The seat of government and administrative capital is La Paz.

The heart of independence beats strongly in the colonial city of Sucre. When the city was founded in 1538, it was named La Plata. The name was later changed to Chuquisaca, and finally to Sucre. Here, in May 1809, the War of Independence from Spain began. In 1840, the city's name was changed to Sucre to honor General Antonio José de Sucre, the first elected president of Bolivia.

Originally, all three branches of government were located in Sucre, but in 1898, the administrative and legislative branches were moved to La Paz. The judicial branch and Supreme Court remained in Sucre. The second-oldest university in South America, the University of San Francisco Xavier, was founded in Sucre in 1624.

Sucre is located at an elevation of 8,530 feet (2,600 m) above sea level. The current population is approximately 207,000. It is the most European of Bolivia's cities. The United Nations selected the city as a Patrimony to Mankind because of its historical and architectural significance.

There are many candidates for the presidency and Congress. For this reason, it is difficult for a single presidential candidate to win a majority of the votes.

In the June 1997 presidential elections, five candidates received most of the votes. Since no candidate had a majority, the Costitution required the Congress to select the new president. The Congress chose General Hugo Bánzer Suárez, who had received 22.3 percent of the vote.

Protecting the Nation

In August 1997, 33,500 men served in the armed forces of Bolivia. Young men may be drafted for one year of military service at the age of eighteen. However, large numbers of draftees are exempted from military duty.

The largest branch of the military is the army, with 25,000 men. Army bases are scattered across the country. Soldiers protect the nation's borders and assist in coca-eradication programs. The air force has 4,000 members, and its planes move supplies around the country. It also does air surveillance for illegal drug activity. Many people are surprised that Bolivia has a navy since it lost its access to the sea in the War of the Pacific. However, 4,500 sailors patrol Lake Titicaca and 8,700 miles (14,000 km) of the nation's navigable rivers.

Bolivia also has a national police force stationed throughout the country. The national police wear green uniforms similar to the army's. These police officers help maintain Bolivia's low crime rate, and they are helpful to tourists. Bolivia is one of the safest places in the world to travel.

La Paz: Did You Know This?

La Paz was founded in 1548 as *Nuestra Señora de La Paz* (Our Lady of Peace). The city is the center of political activity and Bolivia's largest city, with 943,605 residents. The National Palace dominates the city's main square, while San Francisco Church is a center of religious, cultural, and social activity. Construction of the church began in 1549.

La Paz stands at an elevation of 12,000 feet (3,658 meters)—the highest capital city in the world. It is also the only city at that elevation with nearly 1 million residents. La Paz sits in a canyon resembling a football stadium. Houses and apartments cling to the canyon walls, and the central business district is located on the floor of the canyon. The bottom of the canyon is 1,312 feet (400 m) below the surface of the Altiplano. This unusual location protects the city from the bitterly cold winds of the plateau. Residents of La Paz, known as Paceños, love the moderate climate, with temperatures averaging 47°F (8°C) annually.

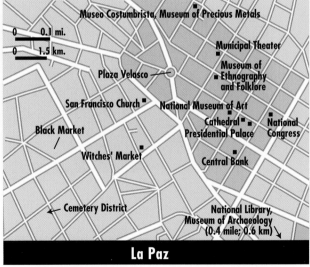

La Paz

Hope for the Future

Opposite: **The historic Silver Mint in Potosí**

A N OLD PROVERB STATES, "DON'T PUT ALL YOUR EGGS in one basket." In economics, that means, "Don't depend on one item of trade to support your national economy." For many years, Bolivia did not heed that advice. From 1545 until the mid-1800s, Bolivia depended on the export of silver. Then, from the late 1800s until the 1980s, the country's economy was dependent on the export of tin. Finally, in the mid-1980s, Bolivia began to diversify its economy. Today, although Bolivia remains a poor country, its economic future appears to be improving rapidly.

Bolivia is the poorest country in South America. In 1998, Bolivians had an average gross domestic product (GDP) of U.S.$2,593. By contrast, the per capita GDP in the United States was U.S.$26,061 and in Canada it was U.S.$18,533. Bolivia is not poor because of a lack of resources, however. With its wealth of natural resources, Bolivia could have been one of the wealthiest nations in the world.

The Silver Era

After silver was discovered at Cerro Rico in 1545, the Spanish colonial government plundered Bolivia's rich natural resource. For 300 years, the Spanish forced the native Bolivians to work in the silver mines under brutal conditions. The Spanish shipped the silver to Spain while the Bolivians suffered and died.

It is estimated that Bolivia produced 70,000 metric tons of silver during that period. The Spanish Crown invested nothing in the development of Bolivia. Instead, they spent the silver on their extravagant lifestyles and costly European wars. So its rich silver deposits did little to improve Bolivia's living conditions.

When the price of silver began to decline in 1865, many Bolivian silver mines closed. Bolivian geologists began to look for a mineral to replace silver. They were fortunate when they discovered huge reserves of tin.

The Tin Era

The discovery of Bolivian tin deposits came at just the right time. In the early part of the twentieth century, world demand

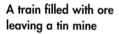
A train filled with ore leaving a tin mine

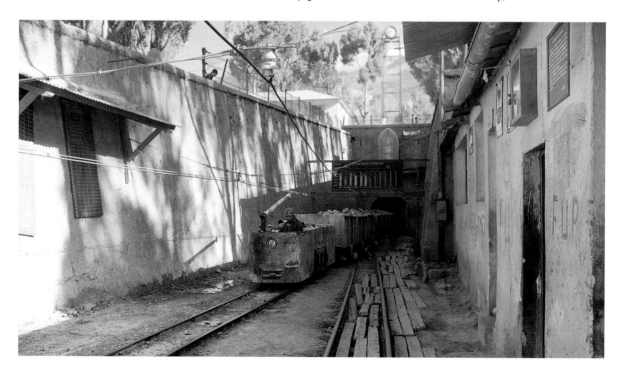

for tin increased dramatically. In 1900, Bolivia supplied 11 percent of world production. By 1921, Bolivia's share of world tin production had increased to 26 percent. The trend continued, and by 1945, Bolivia was producing almost 50 percent of the world's tin.

Many people believe that Bolivia should have become a very rich country because of the sale of tin. Unfortunately, the average Bolivian benefited very little from the export of tin. Three families controlled the tin mines, and they became fabulously wealthy. The three families were the Patiños, the Aramayos, and the Hochschilds. Simón Patiño became one of the world's wealthiest men and lived a life of luxury in Europe. All three families used their wealth to control Bolivian politics and protect their own interests.

By the 1950s, Bolivia had become almost totally dependent on tin exports. The sale of tin provided three-fourths of Bolivia's income. Bolivia had all its economic "eggs" in one basket again. When world tin prices fell, the effect was the same as dropping a basket of eggs. Bolivia's economy was a mess.

During the 1952 Revolution, the Bolivian government nationalized the tin mines. It also began a land-reform program and began to push for variety in the national economy. Today, Bolivia's economy is healthier than it has ever been.

Oil and Gas

One of the brightest lights in the Bolivian economy is the hydrocarbon industry. The eastern lowlands of Bolivia remained sparsely populated and poorly developed until recent

An oil refinery and gas storage facility in Sucre

years. However, discoveries of oil and natural gas in Santa Cruz have changed that situation dramatically. The department of Santa Cruz and its capital, Santa Cruz de la Sierra, are now the economic center of Bolivia. Oil reserves estimated at 200 million barrels have made Bolivia self-sufficient in its petroleum needs.

More important, Santa Cruz is likely to become the hub of a major natural gas distribution network for southern South America. Recent exploration has provided evidence of substantial new gas reserves. Brazilian, Argentinean, and Korean companies have discovered significant new pools of gas at 14,000 feet (4,267 m). These discoveries have pushed estimates of Bolivian gas reserves to 12 trillion cubic feet (340 billion cubic meters).

Because Bolivia has a small national population, the excess natural gas can be sold. Argentina and Paraguay get Bolivian natural gas through pipelines connected to Santa Cruz. However, the major exports in the future will go to Brazil. With a population of more than 170 million, Brazil's appetite for energy seems unlimited.

Recently, Bolivia signed an important agreement to sell Brazil 7 trillion cubic feet (200 billion cu m) of natural gas over the next twenty years. To deliver the gas, a pipeline 1,902 miles (3,060 km) long and 32 inches (81 cm) in diameter was constructed. The pipeline extends from Santa Cruz to the Brazilian state of Rio Grande do Sul. ENRON, a pipeline transmission company based in the United States, was the major investor in the U.S.$1.8-billion project.

Hard Minerals

Bolivia's richest deposits of silver and tin have been mined but important deposits of hard minerals remain. Today, zinc is exported in large quantities. Bolivia also exports tin, silver, tungsten, antimony, gold, and lead.

Environmental damage caused by mining

The mining industry could make a modest recovery over the next few years. Investment capital from foreign companies, new mining equipment and technologies, and improved transportation all offer opportunities for profitable operations.

The major problem facing Bolivia's mining sector is environmental. Hundreds of abandoned mines, refineries, and smelters dot the landscape. Dangerous chemicals, such as mercury, pollute local water supplies. However, the cost of cleaning up past environmental damage is high, and Bolivia is poor. Assistance with environmental programs could come from Western industrial nations that have enjoyed the use of Bolivian minerals.

What Bolivia Grows, Makes, and Mines

Agriculture (1996)

Sugarcane	4,120,000 metric tons
Soybeans	862,000 metric tons
Potatoes	715,000 metric tons

Manufacturing (1994; *value added in U.S.$*)

Petroleum products	$375,000
Food products	$169,000
Beverages	$99,000

Mining (1996)

Zinc	144,764 metric tons
Lead	16,538 metric tons
Tin	14,778 metric tons

Some small farm plots on the Altiplano are irrigated by ancient Inca canals.

Reaping the Harvest

Bolivia's agricultural sector is represented by two vastly different scenes. In the highlands, native Bolivians practice a type of agriculture—subsistence agriculture—that has changed little over time. They grow mainly what they and their families need to survive. They consume 75 percent of what they grow. The other 25 percent is sold to dealers who transport the products to urban markets. Cash sales are small, and the highland Indians are among the poorest people in the world.

Plowing with oxen

Most of the native people have owned their own land since the land-reform program of 1952. Farms are small, and the fields are worked by primitive methods. Crops are cultivated by hand or by using oxen or horses. The soil is thin and of poor quality. Because many Indians plant their crops up and down the slopes, erosion is a serious problem.

The major crop is the potato, a daily staple in the highland diet. Quinoa, a cereal high in protein, is also popular. Several varieties of beans and vegetables are also produced. Sheep and llama are the most common livestock. Their wool is used to produce most of the family's clothing.

Indians make their own clothing and blankets from their sheeps' wool.

Chuño

Chuño, or dehydrated potatoes, are normally prepared in June, when the winter days are sunny and the nights are frosty. The Inca prepared chuño as a food to carry on long treks. Andean Indians still use the same process. Potatoes are spread over the ground and trampled by bare feet to press out the moisture. Then the potatoes lie in the sun and dry. The next morning the process is repeated. When no more moisture remains in the potatoes, they are placed in storage. Chuño maintains its food value for years.

Agricultural practices are quite different in the Oriente, or eastern lowlands. The lowlands provide most of Bolivia's agricultural exports. The department of Santa Cruz is the richest agricultural region of the country. Its vast plains of rich soils and its favorable climate attract many new farmers.

Some of the most successful farmers are Mennonites who migrated to Bolivia from Paraguay. Approximately 38,000 to 40,000 Mennonites farm near the city of Santa Cruz. They are

A Mennonite farm

Inspecting a soybean crop

some of the best farmers in the world. Their farms average 125 acres (50 ha), and the climate allows them to grow two crops each year. The major crop is soybeans, Bolivia's leading agricultural export. They also grow substantial amounts of corn.

The Mennonites are also major dairy farmers. They manufacture a white cheese that is popular throughout Bolivia. They use manure from their dairy cattle to fertilize their fields organically.

Sugarcane, rice, and cotton are also important crops in the lowlands. In the most humid part of the region, ranching replaces crop farming. The department of Beni has more than 3 million cattle. Zebu and Brahma are

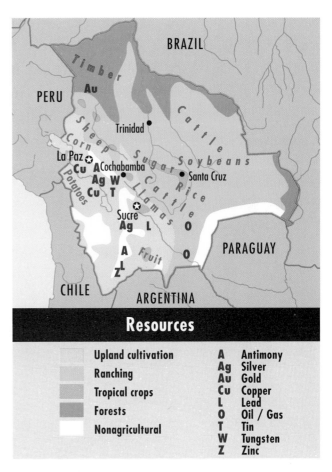

Resources

Upland cultivation	**A** Antimony
Ranching	**Ag** Silver
Tropical crops	**Au** Gold
	Cu Copper
Forests	**L** Lead
Nonagricultural	**O** Oil / Gas
	T Tin
	W Tungsten
	Z Zinc

the most popular breeds. They are resistant to the insects and high temperatures of the Amazon Basin. Beef is the most popular meat in Bolivia.

The Yungas is the primary agricultural region for fruit, coffee, and coca production. The coca plant is used for both legal and illegal purposes. In some years, the product of the coca plant yields more income than any other crop. Currently, Bolivia is working with the United States to eradicate illegal coca plantations.

Expanding Factories

Isolated by mountainous terrain and with no direct access to the sea, Bolivia is just beginning to enter the industrial age. Modern industrial plants are just now emerging. Industrial production is closely related to Bolivia's resources, so one of the most rapidly growing industrial sectors is petrochemicals—chemicals from oil or natural gas. A large oil refinery has been built near Santa Cruz. Plastics, fertilizer, paint, and other chemically related industries are becoming more common.

The refining and smelting of minerals like zinc, tin, lead, and silver

A smelter near Oruro

continue to be important in the mountains. The towering smokestacks of smelters are seen near Potosí and Oruro.

The processing of agricultural products is significant in the major cities. La Paz is the center of textile factories and beer brewing. In Cochabamba, factories process fruits and vegetables. Santa Cruz is represented by modern soybean-processing plants, which ship their products throughout Bolivia and South America. Tarija is the center of a flourishing new wine industry.

Transportation Trauma

The major problem that Bolivia faces in its attempt to enter the global economy is transportation. Trade cannot occur without an adequate transportation network. Most of Bolivia's products are high bulk but low value. To move such products, good highways and railroads are necessary. Bolivia has neither.

Nature has made the building of roads and railroads difficult here. Two parallel ranges of the Andes Mountains with extremely rugged slopes limit east to west movement. Tropical lowlands pelted by heavy rains and floods make road maintenance difficult. The lack of investment capital makes progress slow.

Although Bolivia has 33,035 miles (53,163 km) of roads, only 1,989 miles (3,200 km) are paved. During the rainy season, landslides often block mountain roads. Road surfaces are covered with potholes as big as bomb craters. Hard, dry ridges similar to washboards rattle the teeth of drivers and take a heavy toll on cars. Sometimes people drive in ditches and fields that run parallel to the roads to find a smoother surface.

Poor road conditions make travel through the mountains difficult.

Distance and time are not related. Road conditions are so bad that it can take twelve hours to travel 200 miles (322 km). Driving at a speed greater than 20 miles (32 km) per hour can cause drivers to lose control of their vehicles. If the world community is serious about helping Bolivia develop, wealthy nations must help the nation to create a modern transportation system.

One of the most promising projects is the Ilo Project. In 1992, Bolivia signed a treaty with Peru. The treaty provides Bolivia with a strip of land along Peru's southern border. A new highway from La Paz to Ilo is currently under construction. When the road is completed, Bolivia will have direct access to the Pacific Ocean. If investment capital can be secured, the Bolivians will build a new port at Ilo. The Ilo Project is currently the most important economic development in Bolivia.

Obsolete Railroads

The railroad system is no better than the road system. There are two separate railroad lines. The western line connects the cities of La Paz, Cochabamba, and Oruro with northern Argentina and northern Chile. The eastern line connects the city of Santa Cruz with western Brazil and northern Argentina.

Both lines were built at the turn of the twentieth century using standard British narrow-gauge track, and there has been very little investment in these lines over the past 100 years. Tracks are in need of repair, and engines and railway cars are outdated. The development of an adequate rail system in Santa Cruz Department is necessary for future agricultural growth.

Modern Air Travel

Difficult conditions for ground transportation have led to the expansion of air travel. Bolivia has 693 airports with paved runways. The country also has 248 airports with unpaved runways. These small airports serve the most remote regions of the country. Most of Bolivia's airports have short runways

A small regional airport

serving small single- or twin-engine aircraft. La Paz and Santa Cruz have modern, international airports. Airlines from all over the world fly to these two destinations.

The Capitalization Law of 1994

The most important economic change in Bolivia in recent years took place in 1994. Under the leadership of President Sanchez de Lozada, the government initiated important economic reforms. For many years, Bolivia's national government controlled significant parts of the economy through state ownership. Many state-owned companies were inefficient operations that lost large sums of money.

Sanchez de Lozada convinced the Congress to sell some of the government companies to private investors. The sale allowed foreign investors to own 50 percent of a company. It also gave foreign investors the power to manage a company. The government sold the state airline, railroads, phone company, electrical power companies, and oil company.

The sale of these state-owned companies raised almost U.S.$2 billion. A large portion of this money was used to create a personal social-security account for all Bolivians. These accounts will help to provide for Bolivians when they get older.

The current administration of President Hugo Bánzer is continuing the country's commitment to free-market development. Bolivia is an active member of the Andean community. It is an associate member of MERCOSUR (*El Mercado Común del Sur*, "The Common Market of the South"), a regional trade group founded in the 1990s by Argentina, Paraguay, Uruguay, and Brazil, and it recently joined the World Trade Organization. The government continues to strive to lower inflation and provide a stable environment for foreign investment.

In 1998, Bolivia became the second country in the world to benefit from a special international debt-relief program. The program is called the Heavily Indebted Poor Country (HIPC) debt-relief scheme. If Bolivia continues to improve many of its social conditions, the country will not have to pay back U.S.$450 million it borrowed. Debt reduction and foreign investment are the keys to Bolivia's future economic development.

The 1 Boliviano Coin

Bolivia's currency is the boliviano. One boliviano contains 100 centavos. The 1 boliviano coin is the most commonly used coin in Bolivia. The front side of the coin identifies the coin's value and carries the words *La Union Es La Fuerza* (The Union Is Strength).

The back of the 1 boliviano coin shows the Bolivian coat of arms. It is oval in shape with a complicated design. Cerro Rico Mountain, celebrated for its rich silver deposits, is in the center of the oval. A wheatsheaf, a breadfruit tree, and an alpaca stand beneath the mountain. Above the mountain is a rising sun with a light cloud effect. At the top is the inscription *Bolivia*. On each side of the oval are three Bolivian banners, a cannon, and two rifles with fixed bayonets. An Inca battle-ax is located to the right, and a liberty cap to the left. An Andean condor is perched at the crest of the oval between two branches of laurel and olive.

People Are More than Numbers

BOLIVIA HAS ESCAPED ONE OF THE MOST COMMON PROBlems in the Third World—overpopulation. With an estimated 1998 population of 7,949,933, Bolivia has one of the lowest population densities of any Western Hemisphere country. More people died in the silver mines of Bolivia in the past than live in Bolivia today.

Opposite: **Children on their way to school**

A children's cemetery high in the Andes

Caring for People

Historically, population growth in Bolivia has been limited by a high death rate, largely due to inadequate health care. Sixty percent of the Bolivian people do not have access to proper health care. Many citizens live in isolated areas where there are no doctors or nurses.

In the United States and Canada, people can now expect to live to be seventy-six and seventy-eight years old, respectively. In Bolivia, the average life expectancy is a little less than sixty-two. The infant mortality rate is the second highest in the Western Hemisphere, after Haiti. There are three leading health problems in Bolivia. The greatest is the problem of adequate nutrition; many children suffer

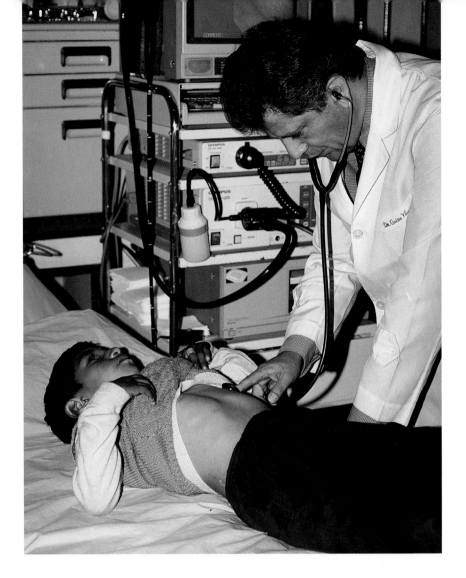

Bolivia needs more health clinics in rural areas.

from protein deficiency. Second, tuberculosis and other respiratory diseases are common. Finally, one of the most common causes of infant death is diarrhea caused by drinking contaminated water.

One of the major tasks facing the Bolivian government today is health care. Rural areas need more clinics, and big-city hospitals for the poor need to be expanded. The World Health Organization and private health-care organizations need to increase their presence in Bolivia.

Mountain Sickness

Soroche, or acute mountain sickness, is a problem for many first-time visitors to Bolivia. The Altiplano is 12,000 to 15,000 feet (3,658 to 4,572 m) above sea level. The air of the Altiplano has 20 to 30 percent less oxygen than the air of the lowlands. Lowland visitors to the mountains often have serious health problems. They may get nauseous, have severe headaches, become dizzy, and even pass out. Visitors should limit their activity for two or three days while their bodies adjust to the elevation.

Native Bolivians have a larger lung volume and extra red blood cells to supply additional oxygen. They also have enlarged capillaries in their hands and feet. This boosts their blood flow and helps keep their hands and feet warm.

Where Are the People?

The average population density for Bolivia is 19 people per square mile (7 per sq km), but the people are not equally distributed. In the Amazon Basin lowlands and the southeastern Chaco, you can travel for miles without seeing anyone. In the highlands around La Paz and El Alto, more than 2 million people are crowded into a small area. As far back as the ancient civilization of Tiwanaku, Bolivians have favored the highlands. Today, six of the country's seven largest cities are located in the highlands. Santa Cruz is the one exception and its population surpassed 1 million in the year 2000.

Many people predict that Bolivia will experience a major population shift over the next fifty years. They believe that residents of old mining centers and

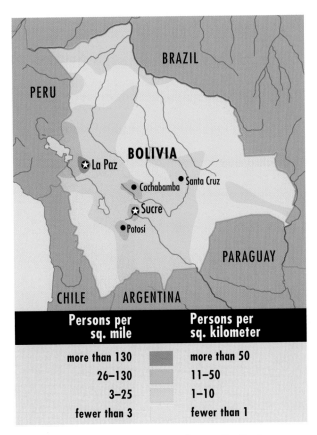

Population distribution in Bolivia

Santa Cruz	951,868
La Paz	943,605
Cochabamba	573,854
El Alto*	534,466
Oruro	238,913
Sucre	207,381

*El Alto is a La Paz suburb, so the La Paz metropolitan area has a population of nearly 1.5 million.

highland farmers will move out of the mountains and onto the plains. Indeed, that process has already begun. It is not uncommon to see highland Indians from Oruro or Potosí selling Chiclets chewing gum on Santa Cruz streets. They appear sadly out of place wearing their traditional heavy woolen clothing in a hot, steamy, tropical environment.

The First Inhabitants

Bolivia has a larger percentage of Native American, or Indian, people than any other country in Latin America. These original people make up 55 percent of the nation's population. Most have remained in the highlands, where they farm for a living. The two major groups of Indian people are the Quechua, who account for

A Quechua man

An Aymara woman and baby

30 percent of the population, and the Aymara, who make up 25 percent. Both groups are independent, self-sufficient, and traditional. The Quechua appear to be a little less resistant to change. They are more outgoing and a little less serious.

The two groups seldom intermarry. The Aymara are believed to be descendants of the great Tiwanakan culture, but they have little sense of their past. The Quechua are connected to the Inca Empire and have a proud sense of their history. Both groups have remained somewhat isolated from Spanish culture. They have preferred not to marry Europeans.

Prior to the 1952 Revolution, Indians had few rights in Bolivia. Voting restrictions required that voters be literate or be property owners. As a result, few Indians could qualify to vote. After the 1952 Revolution, the government allowed anyone over the age of twenty-one to vote. Indians who could not read or write and who did not own property could now participate in elections. There was also important agricultural reform that returned native lands to their rightful owners—the Indians.

One of the most recent examples of political awareness among the native people occurred in 1990. Seven hundred Indians from the town of Trinidad marched thirty-two days and 400 miles (644 km) to La Paz to demand recognition of their land rights. The government responded positively. They acknowledged Indian rights to 3.9 million acres (1.6 million ha) of tropical rain forest in northern Bolivia. They also established a commission to draft a new law for Indigenous Indians of the East and Amazonia.

Most mestizos and Bolivians of pure European ancestry live in the cities.

European Influence

Thirty percent of Bolivia's population are mestizos. A mestizo is a mixture of Indian and European races. Most mestizos live in the cities with the people of pure European ancestry. These European descendants account for about 13 percent of the population. Most are Spanish, but there are small groups of Germans, Italians, Yugoslavians, and Lebanese.

An interesting cultural split exists among the mestizos and whites who live in Bolivia. Those who live in the highlands are termed *Kollas*. They are traditionally more conservative and dress in blacks and grays. They are serious, hardworking, and speak precise Spanish.

Their tropical counterparts are known as *Cambas*. Their favorite city is Santa Cruz. They are more carefree and fun loving. They use more slang, talk faster, and dress in bright colors. Many Cambas like racy cars, salsa music, and spicy foods. A kind of natural competition exists between the two regions, and the Cambas appear to be winning for now.

An African Bolivian

The Africans

One of the more interesting minorities is the African population of the Yungas. They account for about 1 percent of the national population. These black Bolivians are descendants of slaves who escaped from mining camps. Fleeing slavery and certain death, they made their way to the lush tropical regions of Bolivia. Here, they developed successful agricultural pursuits.

Multiple Tongues

Bolivia is the only country in Latin America with three official languages— Spanish, Quechua, and Aymara. Many citizens speak only one of these languages, and at least 30 to 40 percent do not speak Spanish. The Indians were good at teaching

Quechua Riddles

Riddles

1. *P'unchawpas tutapas mana chakiyuq puriq.*
   (Day or night, it never walks on feet.)
2. *Ima k'urun wiksaykita qachun?*
   (What bites you inside your stomach?)
3. *Saqtan, qimpim, yanun, mikun.*
   (You knock him down, then roll up his sleeves, before you cook and eat him.)

Answers

1. *Mach'aqway* (Snake)
2. *Yarqay* (Hunger)
3. *Chojllo* (Corn on the cob)

the Spaniards their languages, but the Spaniards did not do a good job of teaching the Indians Spanish.

Education has been hindered by language because, until recently, all textbooks and teaching were in Spanish. Learning was very difficult for rural students who did not speak Spanish. Textbooks are now being written in Quechua and Aymara, however, and teachers are allowed to use any of the three official languages in the classroom. Most official business and commerce is conducted in Spanish.

Speaking without Words

Body language is an important part of Bolivian life. When women meet, they frequently kiss each other on each cheek while touching each arm. Men greet each other with a warm *abrazo*. The abrazo consists of a firm hug, a handshake, and several pats on the shoulder. Patting on the shoulder is a sign of friendship. If a Bolivian's hands are wet or dirty, he will extend his arm or elbow for greeting. Big smiles are an important part of greetings.

Bolivians also use their eyes, hands, and facial expressions to communicate. When talking to a Bolivian, eye contact is essential. Avoiding another person's eyes is considered an insult. When parents beckon their children, they will wave their fingers with the palm down. A raised hand, with the

The Color of Language

English	Spanish	Quechua	Aymara
red	*rojo*	*puka*	*wila*
green	*verde*	*q'omer*	*ch'ojjna*
blue	*azul*	*anqas*	*sajuma*
yellow	*amarillo*	*k'ello*	*k'ellu*
white	*blanco*	*yuraq*	*jank'o*
black	*negro*	*yana*	*ch'yara*
brown	*moreno*	*ch'umpi*	*ch'umphi*

palm outward and fingers extended, twisting quickly from side to side means no. This gesture is often used by taxi and bus drivers to indicate that their vehicle is full.

Indian women in La Paz

Rural to Urban Migration

One of the major population changes in Bolivia is the growth of cities. Fifteen years ago, more than half of Bolivia's citizens lived in rural areas. Today more than 65 percent live in urban areas. The move from the country to the cities is known as rural to urban migration.

People leave the countryside in hopes of improving the quality of their lives. It is difficult for them to support their families on small farms. The soil is poor. Sometimes frost kills their plants and on other occasions there is not enough rain. Survival is a challenge.

People Are More than Numbers **91**

Some new arrivals to the city build shacks out of tarps.

When they move to the city, people have great hope for a better future. They believe they will get a job and earn money. They hope that their children will receive a better education and improved health care. Sometimes they are successful, and sometimes they are disappointed.

People arriving in the cities often find it difficult to rent a home. Many times, they build a shack out of plywood, tarps, linoleum, and even cardboard. The slum areas where these shacks are built are called *favelas*. Frequently, they have no electricity, running water, or sewage-disposal services.

Later, these newcomers may be able to build a brick house. The city governments try to provide the necessary services, and gradually, their lives improve. Most of these new residents have no desire to return to the country. The La Paz–El Alto area and Santa Cruz are the fastest-growing urban concentrations. El Alto is called a "sleeping city." Its residents sleep in El Alto and ride buses to La Paz to work in factories, stores, and homes.

The Goal of Learning

Improving the quality of education in Bolivia is one of the government's major objectives. The country now spends more than 20 percent of its national budget on education, and more than 83 percent of all Bolivians can read and write today.

Children start school at age six. They continue their primary education for eight years. Federal law requires that

Quechua and mestizo schoolchildren in the Altiplano

children attend school through the primary years. In some rural areas, however, children drop out to help with farmwork. Because of the isolated location of some schools, attendance is sometimes difficult to enforce.

Secondary school begins at age fourteen and lasts four years. A secondary education is not compulsory. In 1999, only 40 percent of these children were attending high school. All elementary and secondary education is free.

There are eight state universities and two private universities in Bolivia. Some have prestigious historical records and are internationally recognized. The University of San Francisco Xavier in Sucre, founded in 1624, is the second-oldest university in South America. San Andre's University is the major public university in La Paz and has the largest student enrollment of all Bolivian universities.

The most modern university in Bolivia, located in Santa Cruz, is the Universidad Privada de Santa Cruz de la Sierra. It was founded on March 12, 1984, because the rapid development of the Department of Santa Cruz required a university that could produce graduates to serve its needs. The university already has more than 2,000 students. In the next ten years, the university could admit 10,000 students. Modern classrooms and the latest technologies are available to eager young students. The university specializes in programs in business, engineering, architecture, computers, and urban and environmental legislation. Businesses are hiring these graduates as quickly as they finish. The university appears to be developing a reputation as one of the best schools for technology in Latin America.

A classroom in the
Universidad Privada
de Santa Cruz

People Are More than Numbers   **95**

Modern Beliefs, Ancient Rites

G OD, GLORY, AND GOLD. SOME HISTORIANS HAVE quoted these three "Gs" to explain Spanish exploration in the New World. The Spanish certainly brought their Roman Catholic religion with them to Bolivia. Cathedrals with towering domes and gold and silver altars grace many cities. Indeed, 95 percent of Bolivians profess to be Catholics. However, as many as half of all Bolivians still practice ancient rites and mix their traditional religious beliefs with Catholicism.

Religions of Bolivia

Catholic	95%
Protestant	5%

Traditional Practices

Many people believe that when the Spaniards arrived in Bolivia, they found a society that did not believe in a Supreme Being, but this is not true. The Aymara and Quechua both had sophisticated religions, which they had practiced for centuries. Their vision of the universe was divided into three layers.

The first layer was the heavens. It was called the *Alajpacha*. This layer was where Viracocha, the creator god, lived. It was also the home of the sun, moon, rain, stars, and thunder and wind. The Inca called the sun god *Inti* and the moon god *Quilla*.

The second layer was the earth—the *Acapacha*. This was the space where humans lived. The *Pachamama* (Mother Earth) controlled this space. The Pachamama tried to harmonize all opposites. Offerings to the Pachamama are still important today. Coca leaves, alcohol, cigarettes, and other gifts are given when praying for good crops, good health, and safe travel. Even in the homes of Catholics of European descent, a few drops of wine or beer are poured on the ground before a toast. It is a tradition to offer the Pachamama the first sip.

The final layer is the Earth's inside space, the *Manqhapacha*. This layer is below the surface of the Earth, and it represents destructive forces and death. Earthquakes and a lack of soil fertility live here with evil spirits and the devil.

The Aymara and Quechua were easily converted to Catholicism. The Indians were practical people, and the Christian doctrines had little meaning for, or influence on, them. They simply incorporated the new Catholic beliefs into

Inside a country church

The Winter Solstice Celebration

Each year, the highland Indians hold an ancient celebration on the first day of winter (June 22–24; dates vary from year to year). The ceremony honors the first rays of the sun for the new year. Both a Catholic mass and pagan rituals are performed. God, or *Inti*, is asked to provide fertility and good luck for the next year's crops. Sometimes a snow-white llama is sacrificed. Its blood is poured on the ground and its hooves and head are buried as an offering to the Pachamama. The major ceremony is held on Isla del Sol in Lake Titicaca. The Incas believed this is where the sun god placed the first Incas on Earth.

their old religion. The religion they adopted was much different than orthodox Catholicism of course. The Catholic God was associated with the sun, the Virgin Mary was compared to the Pachamama, and the Catholic saints were linked with mountain spirits. When the Indians prayed to the saints, they were also communicating with the traditional spirits. Their conversion satisfied the Spanish priests, and their own practice of religion met their needs.

The Church of San Francisco
in La Paz

Monuments to God

Large cathedrals and churches were constructed soon after Bolivian towns were founded. Located on the central plaza, or *zocalo*, many still dominate the central city. The Church of San Francisco in La Paz was begun in 1549, and the Cathedral of Sucre was completed in 1566.

After silver was discovered in Potosí, many wealthy miners contributed to the construction of religious buildings. The Convent of Saint Teresa has a stunning gold altar and a fine collection of sixteenth- and seventeenth-century art. The facade of the Church of San Lorenzo is the most famous example of baroque/mestizo architecture in Bolivia. The intricate stone carvings look like fine lace work.

Intricate stone carvings of
the Church of San Lorenzo
in Potosí

The Missions

Some of the most interesting work of Catholic missionaries took place in the Amazon lowlands of Chiquitos. Chiquitos is a province in the Department of Santa Cruz. Jesuit missionaries from Paraguay established Mission San Javier there in 1691. Later, they founded five more missions in Chiquitos.

The missions were planned cities. In the center of each mission was a large plaza. Around this plaza, the missionaries constructed the church and a priest's house. Homes were also built for the Indian *caciques* (chiefs). A general store, workshops, a jail, and a cemetery were also built. The Indians were encouraged to leave the countryside and settle at the mission sites.

The missions served two major purposes. They allowed the priests to carry out their missionary work, and they protected the Indians from the harsh treatment and exploitation of the Spanish conquistadores. Even though the missionaries directed each mission, Indian chiefs elected by the people governed it. They were allowed to keep their own language and follow their own customs.

The buildings were constructed of precious tropical woods. Beautiful wood carvings and ornate paintings by the Indians have been faithfully restored in recent years. Jesuit priests and, later, Franciscan friars allowed the natives to incorporate their beliefs into Catholicism.

Mission San Javier has an oak carving of Saint Francis of Assisi. In the carving, Saint Francis is surrounded by animals and plants that are typical of the surrounding jungle. The carving represents the love and respect for nature so common

Mission San Javier was established in 1691.

to the followers of Saint Francis. It also represents the Indians' view of the significance of nature in their religious world.

The lowland missions are true jewels of the colonial period, a striking testimony to the Spaniards' obsession with converting the Indians to Catholicism. The United Nations has declared the missions a National Monument and Cultural Patrimony of Mankind.

The Pilgrimage

The Basílica de Nuestra Señora de la Candelaria in Copacabana is the most important pilgrimage site in Bolivia. This sparkling white Moorish-style cathedral overlooks the peaceful shores of Lake Titicaca. Construction was begun in the sixteenth century and ended in 1820.

Inside the cathedral, in a separate chapel, stands a statue of the Virgin of Candelaria. The figure is encased in a gold and silver chamber and is reputed to have the power to heal. During *Semana Santa* (Holy Week), thousands of Bolivians attempt to walk from La Paz to Copacabana to reaffirm their faith.

The journey of 98 miles (158 km) is made at an elevation above 12,000 feet (3,658 m). The trip is difficult, and many pilgrims drop out from fatigue. Those who continue frequently develop blisters on their feet so severe that their shoes fill with blood. Rural Indians sit along the road with pans of hot saltwater to soak the weary pilgrims' feet. As the pilgrims enter the chapel, local residents applaud their efforts. Overcome with emotion, many pilgrims collapse in tears inside the chapel.

Evangelicals

Although Protestants account for only 5 percent of the Bolivian religious community, their numbers are rapidly increasing. The Evangelical denominations are the most active. It is not uncommon to see small adobe Protestant chapels in the most remote regions of Bolivia.

Natural Healing

Bolivia is the only country with a university that offers a degree in natural medicine. In 1988, at the Natural Medicine World Congress in Mexico, Bolivia was declared the cradle of natural medicine.

High in the Andes Mountains near Lake Titicaca live the *Kallawayas*, healers and masters of natural medicine. The

Kallawaya healers

Kallawayas have long been recognized for their holistic approach to medicine. They emphasize that a healthy mind and spirit are essential for physical health and well-being.

The Kallawaya were the medical doctors to the Inca. Their practice was shrouded in mystery by the fact that they spoke a secret language. Only men practiced medicine, and they did not share their secret language with the tribal women. They performed brain surgery before the Egyptians did. In addition, they used more than 200 plants and natural products to aid in healing.

For centuries, the secrets of the Kallawaya healers have been handed down from father to son. Today, however, few young men are following in the footsteps of their fathers. It is possible that the skills of the Kallawaya in natural healing and psychic treatment will be lost with the next generation.

Kallawaya Remedies

- Kaolin clay to calm bowels
- Quinine for fever
- Spiderwebs to stop bleeding
- Bee venom for arthritis
- Heat to remedy the chills
- Avoid cold drafts
- Toasted pellets of llama dung to treat stomach cramps
- Music heals, especially the flute and drums

Strange Powers

Many Bolivians are superstitious. Some believe that the future can be predicted by reading coca leaves thrown on a blanket. In rural areas, farmers will not permit visitors to take photos of their oxen. They believe that every time someone looks at the photo, some of the animal's strength is lost.

Miners at Potosí's Cerro Rico silver mines continue to engage in a unique ceremony before entering the mine. An altar with a cross stands at the entrance. There, miners offer gifts of coca leaves, tobacco, and alcohol to God for his protection.

Dried llama fetuses for sale in the Witches' Market

A little lower in the mine stands a clay statue of the devil (*Tío Sopay*). He has a beard, goat horns, and a solid silver heart. Here, the miners are about to enter the underworld, which is controlled by the devil. Separate offerings of coca leaves, tobacco, and alcohol are made to the devil. The miners ask for his protection and help in finding a pure vein of silver.

In La Paz, behind the Church of San Francisco, there is a Witches' Market. Customers can buy amulets, good-luck charms, and dried llama fetuses. Llama fetuses are often buried beneath new construction projects to drive away evil spirits.

The Good Things of Life

I T HAS BEEN SAID THAT THERE IS A FIESTA SOMEWHERE IN Bolivia every day. The Bolivians are a passionate people who express their joy through music and dance. Frequently, large amounts of food and alcohol are part of the celebrations. Unrestrained behavior is acceptable as long as it remains positive.

Opposite: **Bolivians express their joy through music and dance.**

Fiestas

Most Bolivian fiestas are religious or political. They may be held to honor a Christian or Indian saint, a famous battle, or the revolution for independence. In addition to national holidays, all nine departments have a special day of celebration. Cities, both large and small, have their own fiestas.

Carnival

Carnival is celebrated nationwide during the week before Lent. Participants in the parades and dances may spend an entire year preparing their costumes. Carnival activities have distinct regional differences. The most famous of all Carnival celebrations is in Oruro.

Oruro's population of 238,913 swells to more than 1 million people during the festivities. Known as the "Folkloric Capital of Bolivia," the city is one of the most colorful places in South America

National Holidays in Bolivia	
New Year's Day	January 1
Carnival	Four days before Ash Wednesday
Good Friday	Friday before Easter
Labor Day	May 1
Corpus Christi	Date varies
Independence Day	August 6
All Saints' Day	November 1–2
Christmas Day	December 25

Las Diabladas in Oruro

to spend Carnival. The festival is called *Las Diabladas* (Devil Dances). The costumes and masks are decorated in brilliant colors. The dancers wind through the streets accompanied by the music of guitars, charangos, flutes, and drums. There are several different dances, but most poke fun at the Spanish colonial rulers. Historically, the dances provided a way for the Indian people to protest their treatment by the Spanish colonizers. Visitors can expect to be pelted by water balloons during the celebrations.

The Sounds of Music

Music has always provided an outlet for cultural expression. In Bolivia, musical traditions are noticeably regional. In the Andes and the Altiplano, the musical sounds are haunting and mournful, reflecting the desolate nature of the environment. For centuries, Aymara musicians have used *sampones* (reed panpipes) to recreate the sad sounds of the wind.

In Tarija, the use of violins, guitars, canes, and *cajas* (small drums) produce a warm, happy music. Santa Cruz is the salsa capital, with music that has a strong Brazilian influence.

The music of the Yungas reflects the rhythm and beat of African culture. The *charango*, one of the most popular musical instruments in Bolivia, resembles a small guitar. Its average length is only 25 inches (64 cm), and it has ten strings. Almost all musical groups that play traditional Bolivian music have a charango player.

The city of Aquile, high on the Altiplano, claims to be the birthplace of the charango. Originally, the body of the instrument was made from an armadillo shell. Today, it is more likely to be made from precious Bolivian hardwoods.

The charango resembles a small guitar.

Celebrating Food

Food is not only an important part of daily life, it is the central part of Bolivian fiestas. In the rural highlands, where the potato is the staple food, meals are somewhat bland. However, in the lowlands and urban centers, the food is varied and exciting.

Bolivians are true meat lovers. Their dishes include beef, pork, poultry, and lamb. One of their favorite dishes is the *empanada salteña* (meat pie). Cooks use a mixture of diced meat, chives, raisins, diced potatoes, chopped peppers, and a rich, hot, sweet sauce. These ingredients are then baked in a bread-dough shell.

Chicha

The most popular drink of the average Bolivian is chicha beer (pronounced CHEE-cha). It is made from fermented corn and is quite strong. Drinking chicha beer while driving frequently results in accidents. It is the beverage of choice in rural areas and at fiestas. Chicha beer is often made and sold from people's homes. Along the roads of Bolivia, a long pole with a white flag marks houses with chicha beer for sale.

Tradition states that Bolivians can identify foreigners by the way they eat their empanadas salteña. A true Bolivian will take a small bite out of the corner of the salteña, then sip the sauce out of the small opening. If not a single drop of salsa drops on the plate, the muncher must be Bolivian.

One of the most exciting places to eat in Bolivia is in any city's central market. The markets always have a special area where individual food booths line the aisles. Hungry shoppers have several selections to choose from, such as boiling pots of *api*. Api is a thick, rich drink produced by mashing corn into a paste. Hot water, sugar, and cinnamon are added to produce a rich and nutritious beverage. Other booths offer pork that is deep-fried in vats over open fires. All kinds of sausages, pastries, and breads are available.

In the lowlands, rice, fish, and yucca are common dishes. In Santa Cruz, thousands of weekend visitors eat at kiosks at the Río Pirai recreational area. One of the most popular dishes is yucca. The yucca is pounded

Yucca is a popular food in the lowlands.

into a paste, seasoned, and mixed with cheese. This dough is then wrapped around a wooden stick and cooked over charcoal. Delicious!

The Fashion World

Most European descendants and mestizos dress in Western-style clothes, but the Indians, particularly the women, still cling to their traditional style of dress. Highland Indian women are noted for their long *polleras* (skirts). The skirts are tight at the waist and flow outward to a wide bell shape below the knee. The skirts are composed of several layers with each layer more beautiful than the next.

Hats are an important mark of social status among native women. The colors are usually conservative—shades of blacks and browns. They come in many different shapes. The bowler-type hat is the most popular. If the hat is perched on the side

An elderly woman in traditional dress

Highland girls on their way to school

A mother and son in hand-made clothing. The baby is wearing a chullo.

of the head, the woman is single. If it is perched on top of the head, she is married. Some women have been known to change the position to suit their purpose!

Indian men have adopted most Western clothing styles but many highland men still wear hand-knitted, woolen caps with earflaps. The caps are called *chullos*. Men frequently knit the caps themselves. The colors and designs in the caps identify the region the person comes from.

A Creative Culture

The art and architecture of Bolivia can be traced back many centuries. The Tiwanakan and Inca cultures produced buildings and carvings that have withstood the ravages of time. These ancient civilizations also produced exquisite gold and silver jewelry. Their works in ceramics, textiles, and wood can be seen in many museums. Several of their designs and techniques were incorporated into colonial artwork and architecture.

The Golden Paintbrush

Nicknamed the "Golden Paintbrush," Melchor Pérez Holguín was born in Cochabamba in 1660. When he was eighteen, he opened a studio in Potosí. He painted there for the rest of his life. The people in his paintings were noted for their harsh facial expressions. Deeply set eye sockets, high cheekbones, and sharp noses were standard features. His depiction of robes on priests and monks was so delicate that the fibers of the cloth appeared real. Mythical characters, such as angels, were represented by softer faces and pale, delicate skin colors. The largest collection of Holguín paintings in the world is in the restored Mint of Potosí.

Marína Núñez del Prado

Sculptor Marína Núñez del Prado was born in La Paz in 1910. When she died in 1995, the nation mourned the loss of a great talent. Her work was inspired by Indian themes, characterized by rolling curves and large bulk. She specialized in the use of spectacular materials. Sometimes she carved native Bolivian woods; for other works she used black granite, alabaster, basalt, or white onyx. Two of her most popular pieces—*White Venus* and *Mother and Child*—were sculpted in white onyx.

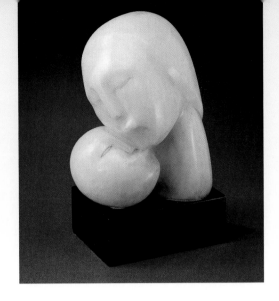

The colonial period produced some of Bolivia's most noted artists. Oil paintings of religious subjects and portraits of famous and powerful people were the most common. Potosí, with its fabulous silver wealth, became the economic, social, and cultural center of the Americas. Wealthy miners supported early painters like Francisco Lopez de Castro and Francisco Herrera y Velarde. However, Melchor Pérez Holguín was recognized as the most outstanding painter in the world representing the Hispano-American baroque style.

The colonial period also yielded some beautiful stone sculptures. Tito Yupanqui, a Bolivian native, sculpted *Our Lady of Copacabana* in 1576. During the seventeenth century, Diego Quispe Curo produced the haunting *Cristo Atado a una Columna* (Christ Tied to a Column).

The twentieth century produced many fine Bolivian artists. Among others, Guzman de Rojas, Arturo Borda, María Luisa Pacheco, Víctor Cuveas Pabon, and Antonio Sotomayor stand out. One of Bolivia's most beloved twentieth-century sculptors is Marína Núñez del Prado.

Soccer Mania

No sport arouses the passions of Bolivians more than *fútbol* (soccer). Even the smallest rural communities have a soccer field. A soccer ball tucked under an arm is a common sight across Bolivia.

Soccer has been played competitively in Bolivia since the first team was organized in Oruro in 1896. Other towns soon formed their own teams. In 1914, Bolivia's first organized league was founded in La Paz. In 1926, Bolivia joined the South American Soccer Federation and began to play in international competition.

Bolivia was one of only thirteen nations that participated in the first World Cup tournament in Uruguay in 1930. The Bolivian team was invited back to the World Cup in 1950. Defying the odds, Bolivia qualified for the World Cup Finals in 1994.

One of the proudest moments in Bolivian sports history came in 1963. In the 1963 America's Cup, Bolivia defeated Brazil in the final game. The America's Cup is South America's most important soccer tournament, so joyous celebrations erupted across the country. The team's players, including Wilfredo Camacho, became instant national heroes.

Bolivia (green) playing Spain in the 1994 World Cup

The fact that Bolivia, with only about 8 million residents, can compete with Brazil (169,806,557) and Argentina (36,265,463) is significant. It illustrates that commitment, training, and the will to win can overcome numbers. Many of today's outstanding Bolivian soccer players learned their skills at the internationally recognized soccer camp, Tahuichi.

Other Games

Schoolchildren in Bolivia usually play soccer or basketball during recess. They also play a game called *Trumfo*. In Trumfo, a wooden top is sent spinning. While it is spinning, the player guides the top onto the surface of his or her hand. As the top spins, it is tossed at a metal bottle cap on the ground. If the top strikes the bottle cap, it causes the cap to fly off the ground. Players race to see who can knock their bottle cap across the finish line first.

Tahuichi Aguilera Academy

The Tahuichi Aguilera Academy in Santa Cruz has trained more than 150,000 children between the ages of six and nineteen. The program concentrates on building leg strength and endurance, both necessary for soccer. Participants run up sand dunes 100 feet (30.5 m) high at a forty-five-degree angle. They also run 4.5 miles (7.24 km) around the dunes. They end by running in a river against a stiff current in water that is 2 feet (0.6 m) deep. Instructors also teach basic skills to go along with the conditioning.

A Slice
of Life

R OBERTO RUBS HIS EYES SOFTLY AS HE SLOWLY BEGINS to awaken. He can see the flickering light from the kerosene lamp in the kitchen. He can hear his mother preparing breakfast. Soon the aroma of fried potatoes and eggs fills the small bedroom he shares with two brothers and a sister. It is 4:30 A.M., almost time to get up.

Opposite: **A thatched-roof adobe house on Isla del Sol**

Isla del Sol

Roberto sits up in bed and looks out the window. The night sky is clear and a billion stars twinkle in the heavens. The moon casts a golden glow over the mirrorlike surface of Lake Titicaca. In about an hour, the sun will peek over the horizon and softly bathe his island in light. Roberto lives with his family on *Isla del Sol* (Island of the Sun).

Lake Titicaca from the wooded shore of Isla del Sol

Lake Titicaca

Location: The southern border of Peru and the northern border of Bolivia

Elevation: 12,507 feet (3,812 m) above sea level

Length: 110 miles (180 km)

Width: 45 miles (72.4 km)

Depth: 1,499 feet (457 m)

Surface Area: 3,200 square miles (8,290 sq km)

Average Water Temperature: 51°F (10.5°C)

Number of Islands: 36

Interesting Fact: The highest navigable lake in the world

Isla del Sol is not an ordinary island. It is located in one of the world's most famous lakes—Lake Titicaca. The night air is cold. Roberto quickly snuggles back under his cozy llama bedspread. He drifts into deep thought about the special place where he lives.

The First Inca

Roberto remembers the stories his father tells about the past. His father says that Bolivia was once part of one of the world's great empires—the Inca Empire. The empire stretched for 2,500 miles (4,023 km) from Ecuador to Chile. The Inca believed that Isla del Sol was the center of the universe.

No matter how many times Roberto hears the story, he always pleads with his father to repeat the legend of the first Inca. According to his father, the Inca worshiped a god named Viracocha. Viracocha was the creator of the universe. The sun god was his servant. Viracocha instructed the sun god to place the first two Inca in front of a rock on Isla del Sol.

In the Inca language, the rock is called Titikjarka. *Titi* means "puma" or "wild cat" and symbolizes power. *Kjarka* means "rock." Roberto has visited the rock many times. It is located on the north end of the island.

Puma Rock

The first Inca were named Manco Kapac and Mama Ocillo. They were instructed to give their descendants three commandments. The first commandment was *ama sua* (do not steal). The second commandment was *ama lulla* (do not lie). The third commandment was *ama kella* (do not be lazy). The penalty for breaking these commandments was death. Roberto has seen the rock slab where the sinners were sacrificed. He makes a mental note not to break those commandments.

A New Day

"Roberto! José! Felipe! María!" Roberto's thoughts are rudely interrupted by the gruff voice of his father. Bedcovers fly back, and eight feet hit the floor running. When Papá calls your name, it is time to get up!

As Roberto and his brothers and sister enter the kitchen, his father is finishing his second cup of coca maté. Coca maté is a tea made from the coca leaf. The Incas believed that the coca shrub was a sacred plant. Almost all Bolivians drink coca tea. The tea helps offset problems caused by living at high elevations. It calms the stomach, reduces headaches, and provides energy.

Burros carry heavy loads on the island.

All the children rush to their mother for hugs and kisses. She is grinning from ear to ear and her eyes twinkle. Roberto has seldom seen her in a bad mood. Although her life is difficult, she never complains. She has given birth to eight children. Two of the children died at birth because medical facilities on the island are simple. Four children are still at home. The two older children are adults. The oldest sister, Lupita, is married and lives in Copacabana, just across the lake. The older brother, Mario, works in La Paz.

Into the Fields

After breakfast, it is time to go to work. Roberto's family are farmers. They own three dairy cows, fifteen sheep, and one burro. His father also owns seven pieces of land. The fields are small and scattered within easy walking distance of the house. On Isla del Sol, everyone walks. There are no roads, no cars, and no trucks. If they have heavy objects to carry, they use their burros. Before leaving for the fields, they milk the cows and feed the sheep.

Roberto's father grows several different crops. One field produces *aba* (lima beans). Another yields *tarhui* (green beans). He also has a small field of *ardeja* (peas). The largest fields are used to grow potatoes and quinoa. Quinoa is a cereal grain used for flour to make bread. It is also used to thicken soups.

Today, the family will work in the potato fields. They grow seven kinds of potatoes and they eat potatoes at almost every meal. Roberto raises his hoe over his shoulder for the first time at 7:00 A.M. By noon his back is aching. Everyone returns to the house, where his mother has the noon meal on the table. After eating, Roberto lies down for a siesta.

Terraced farm fields

In the afternoon, the family returns to the fields from 2:00 P.M. to 5:00 P.M. By this time, the sun is starting to drop in the sky. It is time to return to the house and take care of the livestock.

A Big Surprise

Tonight, Roberto's mother has prepared a special treat. It is a piece of fried beefsteak served on a bed of rice. In the middle of the steak are two fried eggs. This is Roberto's favorite meal. While he is busy enjoying his supper, his father interrupts him. "Roberto, I want you to do me a big favor tomorrow. The boat from Copacabana is going to deliver a new kerosene lamp for your room. I want you to walk across the island and pick up the lantern."

Roberto can hardly believe his ears. He loves to go down to the dock when the boat comes in. It almost always brings tourists. They come from Japan, Italy, Germany, the United States, Canada, and many other countries. They all want to visit the spot where the first two Inca were placed on Earth. Maybe tomorrow he will get a chance to meet a new friend. By 8:30 P.M., Roberto is in bed.

The Big Day

In the morning, Roberto's father does not have to call him. He is dressed and in the kitchen when his Papá gets up. His father jokes that he wished it was that easy to get him up every morning. A big smile breaks across Roberto's face. He knows that his father could have picked one of his brothers to go for the lantern.

It will take Roberto an hour to walk to the dock. He can't wait to leave. At the last minute, he goes back to his room. When he returns, he is wearing his best white sweater.

As he walks up the path to the top of the island, he turns and looks back. It is a beautiful day. The air is clear and sweet. He can see his adobe house with the thatched roof tucked alongside a peaceful bay. Centuries-old agricultural terraces line the slopes of the island.

He starts down the trail toward the dock and passes a small, new hotel. Change is coming to his island. In the past five years, four hotels have sprouted on the slope facing the dock. This is good news for his father, who sells fresh milk to the hotels.

New hotels are opening on Isla del Sol.

The last part of the trail is steep but it is easy to walk on because it is a stone stairway. It was built by the Inca more than 400 years ago and is still in remarkably good condition. Where the stairway turns for the final approach to the dock, springwater flows from an ancient Inca fountain. The Inca built a stone fountain with three different openings for the springwater. Some people say that the water has three different tastes, one for each hole. Others say the water is a source of eternal youth. Roberto doesn't believe them. There are too many old people on the island.

When the boat arrives, Roberto greets an old friend, Pepe. They are classmates, but Pepe doesn't have to work in the fields. He works as a deckhand on one of the lake's hydrofoils. The hydrofoils are motorboats that ride on a cushion of air across the surface of the water.

Hydrofoils cross the lake on a cushion of air.

Today the boat is packed with tourists, eager to start their adventure. Within minutes the boat is empty, except for the freight. Pepe hands Roberto the carton with the new kerosene lamp, but he is too busy to take time to talk. He has to get the boat ready for the return trip to Copacabana.

Roberto turns and with his shoulders slumped, starts for home. It didn't turn out the way he had hoped. He wanted to meet some tourists.

A New Friend

About halfway up the Inca Stairway, three people are sitting on the side of the steps. Two of the people are a young couple who appear to be Bolivians. The other is an older, gray-haired man who appears to be an American. He is holding a large camera bag and gasping for his breath. It is clear he is not accustomed to the thin air above 12,000 feet (3,658 m).

Although Roberto prefers to speak his native Aymara language, he also speaks Spanish. "*¿Como están?*" (How are you?), he asks. The older man surprises him when he replies, "*muy bien*" (very good) in Spanish. After polite

The Inca Stairway

introductions, they start back up the stairway slowly, talking as they walk. The young couple is from La Paz. The older man is from the United States.

The American wants to know all about life on the island. Roberto answers every question. The man seems to be especially interested in Roberto's education. Roberto tells him that he is fourteen years old. He is the first person in his family to go to high school. He has just completed his freshman year at a school on the north end of the island.

Roberto in his best white sweater

The man wants to know how far he has to walk to school, since there are no roads or buses. Roberto replies, "twelve kilometers." It takes three hours to walk to school. He leaves before daylight. After school, he usually hitches a ride with a local fisherman in his boat. The return trip takes only thirty minutes.

"What do you like to study most?" the man asks. "Mathematics," Roberto blurts out. He tells the man that he wants to study computers in a school in La Paz when he graduates. The American has visited La Paz and thinks it is a very large city. He wants to know if Roberto would like to live and work in La Paz. Roberto tells him, "No, I want to return to my island and work in one of the new hotels." He knows more tourists will be coming each year. He hopes that he can help protect the simple life of the island. But he knows that the tourists will bring money. Perhaps some of the money will be used to improve health care and education on the island.

When they reach the top of the island, Roberto tells the tourists he must return home. Before he leaves, the American reaches in his camera bag. "So you want to study mathematics?" He hands him a brand-new solar-powered calculator. Roberto's eyes open wide. "No," he says, "I could never take something so valuable from a stranger." However, the man insists. "Calculators are very inexpensive in the United States." He tells Roberto that educated young people like him "are the key to Bolivia's future."

A Bridge to the Future

The group parts company with a round of firm handshakes. Roberto's heart is racing as he enters the house. "Mama! Mama! Look what a tourist just gave me." Tears begin to form in his mother's eyes when she sees the calculator. Roberto is a good boy. He will have an education. She did not have that opportunity. She can neither read nor write.

She holds Roberto tightly. He will be a bridge between the past and the future. He will make a difference in Bolivia. She is very proud.

Timeline

Bolivian History

People arrive in Bolivia.	**About 8000–10,000** B.C.
Tiwanaku culture develops, rises, and disappears near Lake Titicaca.	**1600** B.C.–A.D. **1200**
Kollas rule the Bolivian highlands.	**1200–1438**
Inca rule the Bolivian highlands.	**1430s**
Spaniards led by Francisco Pizarro conquer the Inca.	**1532**
Spaniards set up a local administrative center at La Plata, now called Sucre.	**1538**
Indian peasant discovers silver near present-day Potosí.	**1544**
$1.5 billion in silver is sent from Bolivia to the king of Spain.	**1545–1575**
La Paz is founded.	**1548**
University of San Francisco Xavier is founded in Sucre.	**1624**
Potosí has a population of 160,000.	**1650**

World History

2500 B.C.	Egyptians build the Pyramids and Sphinx in Giza.
563 B.C.	Buddha is born in India.
A.D. **313**	The Roman emperor Constantine recognizes Christianity.
610	The prophet Muhammad begins preaching a new religion called Islam.
1054	The Eastern (Orthodox) and Western (Roman) Churches break apart.
1066	William the Conqueror defeats the English in the Battle of Hastings.
1095	Pope Urban II proclaims the First Crusade.
1215	King John seals the Magna Carta.
1300s	The Renaissance begins in Italy.
1347	The Black Death sweeps through Europe.
1453	Ottoman Turks capture Constantinople, conquering the Byzantine Empire.
1492	Columbus arrives in North America.
1500s	The Reformation leads to the birth of Protestantism.

Bolivian History

Bolivia proclaims independence from Spain.	1809
Bolivia is declared a republic after 16 years of warfare with Spain.	1825
Bolivia experiences political instability.	1825–1981
Bolivia's first Constitution is approved.	1826
The price of silver begins to decline.	1865
Bolivia and Chile fight over rich nitrate deposits in western Bolivia; Bolivia loses its western territory and access to the Pacific Ocean.	1879–1883
Tin replaces silver as major export.	1920s
Bolivia fights a war with Paraguay and loses the Chaco territory.	1932–1935
Víctor Paz Estenssoro, leader of the Nationalist Revolutionary Movement, serves as president and brings about political reforms.	1952–1956
Estenssoro again serves as president.	1960–1964
Ernesto (Ché) Guevara tries to bring about a revolution but is captured and killed; major changes are made in Bolivia's Constitution.	1967
General Luis Garcia Meza seizes power in a violent coup.	1980
Estenssoro serves as Bolivia's president for the third time and begins economic reforms.	1985–1989
Under President Sanchez de Lozada, the government sells some of its companies to private investors.	1994
General Hugo Bánzer Suárez assumes the presidency.	1997

World History

1776	The Declaration of Independence is signed.
1789	The French Revolution begins.
1865	The American Civil War ends.
1914	World War I breaks out.
1917	The Bolshevik Revolution brings Communism to Russia.
1929	Worldwide economic depression begins.
1939	World War II begins, following the German invasion of Poland.
1957	The Vietnam War starts.
1989	The Berlin Wall is torn down, as Communism crumbles in Eastern Europe.
1996	Bill Clinton is reelected U.S. president.

Fast Facts

Official name: República de Bolivia (Republic of Bolivia)

Capitals: Sucre is the official capital; La Paz is the actual capital and Bolivia's largest city

La Paz

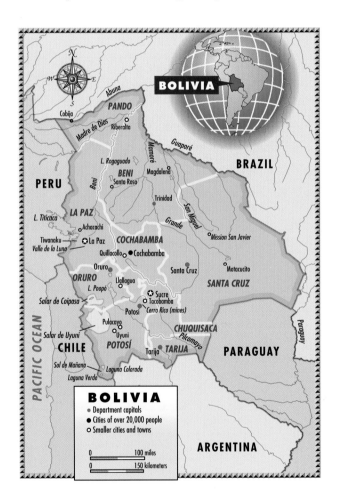

Bolivia's flag

Salar de Uyuni

Official languages: Spanish, Quechua, and Aymara

Official religion: About 95% of the people are baptized Roman Catholic but many continue to honor traditional beliefs

Year of founding: 1825

National anthem: *Bolivianos, el hado propicio* ("Bolivians, the Propitious Fate")

Government: Republic

Chief of state: President

Head of government: President

Area and dimension: 424,165 square miles (1,098,587 sq km)
Length east—west: 800 miles (1,287 km)
Length north—south: 900 miles (1,448 km)

Coordinates of geographic center: 17° S, 65° W

Bordering countries: Brazil to the north and east; Peru and Chile to the west; Argentina and Paraguay to the south

Highest elevation: Mount Sajama, 21,463 feet (6,542 m) above sea level

Lowest elevation: Southeastern border with Paraguay, 300 feet (91 m) above sea level

Average temperature: 80°F (27°C) in the lowlands;
47°F (8°C) in the highlands

Average annual rainfall: 60 inches (152 cm) in the tropical lowlands;
10 inches (25 cm) in the Atacama

National population (1998): 7,949,933

Lake Titicaca

Currency

Population of largest cities (1998):

Santa Cruz	951,868
La Paz	943,605
Cochabamba	573,854
El Alto	534,466
Oruro	238,913

Famous landmarks:
- ▶ *Amboró National Park*
- ▶ *Basílica de Nuestra Señora de la Candelaria,* in Copacabana
- ▶ *Laguna Colorado*
- ▶ *Laguna Verde*
- ▶ *Lake Titicaca*
- ▶ *Mission San Javier*
- ▶ *National Palace*, La Paz
- ▶ *Noel Kempff Mercado National Park*
- ▶ *Tiwanaku Ruins*
- ▶ *Valley of the Moon*, near La Paz
- ▶ *Witches' Market*, La Paz

Industry: Bolivia is still a nation rich in mineral resources. Oil and natural gas are the nation's most important resources today. Bolivia produces enough oil for its own needs and exports large amounts of natural gas. Zinc, tin, silver, tungsten, antimony, gold, and lead are also mined and exported. Large-scale industrial production is just beginning in Bolivia and is tied to its mineral resources. Santa Cruz has a large oil refinery. Plastics, paint, and fertilizers are other products made from Bolivia's mineral resources.

Currency: The *boliviano* is Bolivia's basic monetary unit. In mid-2000, U.S.$1 = 6.12 bolivianos

Weights and measures: Metric system; however, old Spanish measurements are also used.

Children walking to school

Literacy:	83 percent	
Common Spanish words and phrases:	*adiós* (ah-dee-OHS)	goodbye
	ahuayo (ah-WAH-yoh)	shawl worn by Quechua women to carry babies or produce
	buenos días (BWAHN-ohs DEE-yahs)	good morning
	buenas noches (BWAHN-ahs NOH-chess)	good evening/night
	campesino (KAM-peh-see-noh)	Indian/peasant/ country person
	chullo (CHOO-yoh)	knit hat with ear flaps, worn by men
	¿Cuánto? (KWAHN-toh)	How much?
	¿Cuántos? (KWAHN-tohs)	How many?
	¿Dónde está . . . ? (DOHN-day ess-TAH)	Where is . . . ?
	gracias (grah-SEE-ahs)	thank you
	no (noh)	no
	por favor (pohr fah-VOHR)	please
	sí (see)	yes
	soroche (soh-ROH-chee)	altitude sickness

Simón Bolívar

Famous Bolivians:	Atahualpa *Last of the Inca kings*	(c. 1502–1533)
	Simón Bolívar *South American liberator*	(1783–1830)
	Francisco Herrera y Velarde *Spanish painter*	(1576–c.1656)
	Marína Núñez del Prado *Bolivian sculptor*	(1910–1995)
	Víctor Paz Estenssoro *Founder of the MNR, President of Bolivia*	(1907–)
	Melchor Pérez Holguín *Bolivian painter*	(c. 1660–1724)
	Francisco Pizarro *Spanish conquistador*	(c. 1475–1541)
	Antonio José de Sucre *South American liberator*	(1795–1830)

To Find Out More

Nonfiction

▶ Cobb, Vicki. *This Place Is High: The Andes Mountains of South America. Imagine Living Here.* New York: Walker and Company, 1993.

▶ Ghinsberg, Yossi. *The Harrowing Life-and-Death Story of Survival in the Amazon Rainforest.* New York: Random House, 1993.

▶ Hermes, Jules. *The Children of Bolivia.* Minneapolis: Lerner Publishing Group, 1995.

▶ Rodgers, Mary, and Gretchen Bratvold. *Bolivia in Pictures.* Minneapolis: Lerner Publishing Group, 1987.

▶ Shukman, Henry. *Sons of the Moon: A Journey in the Andes.* Old Tappan, N.J.: Macmillan Publishing Company, 1989.

Articles

▶ Hodgson, Bryan. "Simón Bolívar." *National Geographic*, March 1994, 36–65.

▶ Reinhard, Johan. "Sacred Peaks of the Andes." *National Geographic*, March 1992, 84–111.

▶ White, Peter. "An Ancient Indian Herb Turns Deadly: Coca." *National Geographic*, January 1989, 3–47.

Maps

▶ **Bolivia Color Map**
http://www.lonelyplanet.com.au/ dest/sam/bolivia.htm#pix03
Click on selected geographic locations to access interesting information about the site.

▶ **Bolivia–Country Map**
http://www.lib.utexas.edu/Libs/PCL/
Map_collectionamericas/BoliviaGIF
*An excellent political map showing
regional boundaries, cities, and roads.*

Photos

▶ **Children in Bolivia**
http://www.main.nc.us/ARHC/
children.htm
*High-quality color photos of
Bolivian children.*

▶ **Bolivia Photo Gallery**
http://www.discovery.com/exp/
bolivia/photogallery.html
*Viewers are asked to match animal
names with animal descriptions. When
the answer is right, the animal photo
pops into the ecological setting.*

Websites

▶ **Destination Bolivia**
http://www.lonelyplanet.com/dest/
sam/bolivia.htm
*Information on geography, economics,
culture, government, history, travel,
and ecology.*

▶ **Bolivia Web-Arts and History**
http://www.boliviaweb.com/art.htm
*This site is especially good for art,
literature and music (some bilingual
information).*

▶ **CIA World Fact Book**
http://www.odci.gov/cia/
publications/factbook/bl.html
*Current information on geographic,
economic, political, and social issues
in Bolivia.*

▶ **Culture of the Andes**
http://www.andes.org/riddle.html
*Songs, riddles, stories, vocabulary,
poetry, jokes, and other resources.
Translations of the Quechua language.*

Organizations and Embassies

▶ **Embassy of the Republic of Bolivia**
3014 Massachusetts Avenue, N.W.
Washington, D.C. 20008
(202) 483-4410
*Note: Bolivia also has Consulate
Generals' offices in Los Angeles,
Miami, New York, and San Francisco.*

Index

Page numbers in *italics* indicate illustrations.

Meet the Author

BYRON AUGUSTIN is a professor of geography at Southwest Texas State University in San Marcos, Texas. His love for geography has given him an excellent excuse to travel. He has visited forty-nine of the fifty United States. He has also traveled to twenty-six of Mexico's thirty-one states, as well as eight Canadian provinces. Professor Augustin has visited fifty-four countries on five of the seven continents.

In addition to his travels, he is an avid professional photographer. More than 1,000 of his photos have been published worldwide by the National Geographic Society, Encyclopedia Britannica, *Outdoor Life*, and scores of books and magazines. More than a dozen books in the Enchantment of the World series have featured his photos. He and his wife, Rebecca, coauthored the book *Qatar* in the Enchantment of the World series.

Writing the book on Bolivia was a pure joy. He teaches a course on the geography of Latin America and has been reading about and doing research on Bolivia for more than thirty years. To write this book, he used the superb library facilities

on his own campus. He also surfed the Internet and reviewed 110 years of *National Geographic*. Most of the statistical data were provided by government agencies during his January 1999 visit to Bolivia.

Augustin feels strongly that it is difficult to write about a country without visiting it personally. As a result, he spent two weeks in Bolivia gathering data, interviewing Bolivians, and taking photos for the book. He traveled more than 3,500 miles (5,600 km), in a four-wheel-drive vehicle with two Bolivian companions. He watched the moon rise over Lake Titicaca, slept in a bed carved from salt, descended into the guts of the Cerro Rico silver mine, and took a boat trip down an Amazon tributary. He fell in love with Bolivia and its remarkable citizens.

Photo Credits

Photographs ©:

AllSport USA: 114 (Ben Radford), 9 (Mark Thompson);

Archive Photos: 62 (Reuters), 55 (Rickey Rogers/Reuters), 54, 58;

Art Resource, NY/Giraudon: 50, 133;

Brown Brothers: 45 top;

Byron Augustin: 2, 12 bottom, 21 bottom, 24, 44 top, 71, 72, 75 top, 78, 79, 84, 92, 94, 99, 100 bottom, 102, 110, 111 bottom, 116, 119, 120, 121, 123, 124, 126;

Carl Deal: 83, 105, 109;

Christie's Images: 113;

Corbis-Bettmann: 19 (Barnabas Bosshart), 74 (Bojan Brecelj), 51 (Jeremy Horner), 96 (Julie Houck), 40 top, 117 (Wolfgang Käehler), 32 top (Buddy Mays), 20 top (Rick Price), 45 bottom;

H. Armstrong Roberts, Inc./A. Littlejohn: 111 top;

Liaison Agency, Inc.: 106 (Carlos A. Angel), 21 top, 22, 131 bottom (Bill Cardoni), 52 (Hulton Getty);

National Geographic Image Collection/Maria Stenzel: 73 bottom;

Peter Arnold Inc.: 41 (Oldrich Karasek), 68 (Yoram Lehmann), 16, 20 bottom, 38 (Chlaus Lotscher), 32 bottom, 37 top, 66 (Luiz C. Marigo), 73 top, 98 (Jeffrey L. Rotman);

South American Pictures: 81, 132 bottom (Pedro Martínez), 91, 100 top (Kimball Morrison);

South American Pictures/Tony Morrison: cover, 6, 7 top, 8, 10, 12 top, 14, 23, 25, 28, 28, 29, 30, 33 bottom, 40 bottom, 47 top, 49, 60, 63, 65 top, 70, 86, 87, 93, 104, 108, 130 left, 132 top;

The Image Works: 88 (Richard Lord), 112 (Michael Wickes);

The Image Works/Fotos Bolivia: 56, 57, 76, 82, 89, 133 top (Patricio Crooker), 33 top (Lidia Dávila), 125 (Javier Núñez de Arco), 115 (Selwyn Panigua), 59 (Nicolás Quinteros);

Visuals Unlimited: 7 bottom, 31, 37 bottom (Francis & Donna Caldwell), 36 (Glenn M. Oliver);

Maps by: Joe LeMonnier.